What Christian Leaders *Are Saying about*
Gary V. Whetstone

The level of teaching that [Pastor Gary Whetstone] brings to the table is absolutely incredible! You need this. It's going to take you to the next level. When you get an opportunity to hear something that Pastor Whetstone has endorsed and prepared, you are dealing with somebody who's not just been in the boardroom, but has been right there on the field fighting...and he knows what he's talking about.

—*T. D. Jakes*
Apostle and bishop, The Potter's House, Dallas, Texas

Gary and Faye Whetstone attended our church in Tulsa before they began the powerful work that they now do in Delaware. We're excited for the new Bible training they have, to put God's Word practically into people's lives. They have a vision to reach the world for Jesus Christ. We highly recommend what Gary and Faye Whetstone are doing in this new Bible Study training. Get plugged in!

—*Billy Joe Daugherty*
Founder and pastor, Victory Christian Center, Tulsa, Oklahoma

It's indeed a great honor to talk to you about this incredible biblical study program under the anointed leadership of Gary Whetstone. First, I have known Gary for many, many years. Gary is an incredible pastor and teacher and evangelist to the nations of the world, and is spiritually qualified to head up this marvelous biblical study. I wholeheartedly recommend this biblical study ministry under the leadership of Gary Whetstone.

—*Morris Cerullo*
Founder, World Evangelism, Inc., San Diego, California

I believe that all those who sit under this anointed teaching and the ministry of Pastor Whetstone at this remarkable school will be thoroughly equipped to gather in the end-time harvest before the imminent return of our Lord and Savior Jesus Christ.

—*Rod Parsley*
Pastor, World Harvest Church, Columbus, Ohio

I have been in the pulpits of the world with Gary Whetstone, and I have personally witnessed the anointing and power that God uses through him to literally changes lives. The quality and the depth of his teaching, its interdenominational flavor, and its anointed power is something that I encourage you to take advantage of.

—*Charles Blair*
Late pastor, Calvary Temple, Denver, Colorado

MILLIONAIRE
MENTALITY

MILLIONAIRE MENTALITY

GARY WHETSTONE

WHITAKER
HOUSE

Unless otherwise indicated, all Scripture quotations are taken from the King James Version of the Holy Bible. Scripture quotations marked (AMP) are taken from *The Amplified* Bible, © 1954, 1958, 1962, 1964, 1965, 1987 by The Lockman Foundation. Used by permission. (www.Lockman.org). Scripture quotations marked (NIV) are taken from the *Holy Bible, New International Version*®, NIV®, © 1973, 1978, 1984 by the International Bible Society. Used by permission of Zondervan. All rights reserved. Scripture quotations marked (NKJV) are taken from the *New King James Version*, © 197 1980, 1982, 1984 by Thomas Nelson, Inc. Used by permission. All rights reserved.

Boldface type in the Scripture quotations indicates the author's emphasis.

MILLIONAIRE MENTALITY

Gary Whetstone
P.O. Box 10050
Wilmington, DE 19850
www.gwwm.com
E-mail: info@gwwm.com

ISBN: 978-1-62911-551-1
eBook ISBN: 978-1-62911-573-3
Printed in the United States of America
© 2015 by Gary V. Whetstone

Whitaker House
1030 Hunt Valley Circle
New Kensington, PA 15068
www.whitakerhouse.com

Library of Congress Cataloging-in-Publication Data (Pending)

1 2 3 4 5 6 7 8 9 10 UJ 21 20 19 18 17 16 15

"For as [a man] *thinks in his heart, so is he."*
—Proverbs 23:7 (NKJV)

"But thou shalt remember the LORD *thy God: for it is he that giveth thee power to get wealth, that he may establish his covenant which he sware unto thy fathers, as it is this day."*
—Deuteronomy 8:18

CONTENTS

INTRODUCTION

At the end of the week or month, do you have less money than you need? Does it seem that your purse or wallet contains holes? Do you feel that you never have enough time to work at *and* accomplish everything else you must do? Are you working so hard that you cannot enjoy your earnings? Do you dislike your job and wish you could find the perfect career? Does it seem like a burden to ponder the God-given dream in your heart, because you don't know how to accomplish it? Many people face stressful challenges like these without knowing how to escape the frustration.

As a child, I often heard my father joke on payday that he was putting his paycheck into a "bag with holes." For ten years of my working life, I adopted my father's attitude and followed in his pathway regarding finances. Then, in 1978, I discovered biblical truths that set my finances free!

Do you want to experience freedom in your finances? The Bible promises that God is no respecter of persons: *"Then Peter opened his mouth, and said, Of a truth I perceive that God is no respecter of persons"* (Acts 10:34).

It is God's will for you to discover these biblical secrets. Then you can live in financial freedom, too. Ask yourself, *Am I following similar perspectives of lack? Am I ready for a breakthrough?* If so, this book is for you!

Proverbs 10:22 promises, *"The blessing of the* LORD, *it maketh rich, and he addeth no sorrow with it."*

Do you believe that it is God's will to bless you? Do you realize that His blessing produces wealth with no sorrow?

Imagine your life if you experienced God's promise in Proverbs 10:22. Would you eliminate many activities that produce sorrow and financial frustration in your life? I believe that your life will not be the same when you understand and implement God's principles in your finances.

You see, God's Word contains all-powerful, never-changing principles designed to rule your circumstances. When you align yourself with His Word, you will be perpetually blessed and experience freedom in every area of life. In this book, we will study the progression of financial principles in the Bible, which form what call the "millionaire mentality." These are *purpose, prophetic vision, pregnant meditation, proclamation,* and *provision.*

As you read these pages, I pray that God will inspire you with clear answers about how to achieve His dreams in your heart. Get ready to embark on an exciting journey to personal fulfillment and biblical prosperity!

1

BIRTH THE MILLIONAIRE MENTALITY

It took a Jewish lawyer for God to get my attention. Since then, my business and personal life has never been the same. The simple revelation I received from God one day revolutionized my perspective and birthed the millionaire mentality. I believe it will do the same for you!

It all began in 1978 when my wife, Faye, and I started a small business with only one thousand dollars and a desire for freedom from the everyday working world. From our home, we started selling woodstoves to several friends and coworkers. Because the United States was in the midst of an energy crisis, oil prices were so high that people were turning to alternative fuels to heat their homes. Within two years, to our amazement, we owned five corporations with total gross sales of ten million dollars! With three retail stores, a thriving wholesale business, and a manufacturing-representative business, we were on the verge of launching our own franchise business.

At this point you might be thinking, *It's no wonder that you could think like a millionaire, because of all you had.* But appearance is not necessarily reality, so don't jump to any conclusions yet!

You see, on most days, my wife and our staff worked tirelessly from 5:00 A.M. until 11:00 P.M. Soon, the businesses, which I had formed to bless my family, consumed us. The huge amount of work required was quickly becoming a burden. I found myself serving the very thing that I had created.

Something had to change, but I didn't know what. That's when God intervened in a very unexpected way—through a Jewish woman.

WHO PLANTED THE GARDEN OF EDEN?

During those years, I retained a tax lawyer to assist in decision-making regarding our general business operations. She was a Jew, and I was a Christian. As you might expect, I continually witnessed to her about accepting Jesus Christ and becoming saved However, at one of our meetings, instead of my words changing her life, this Jewish lawyer made a statement that completely revolutionized *my* life!

I pray that you will hear what I heard that day. In fact, encourage you to take a moment to pray before you read any further. Ask God to give you ears to hear, in Jesus' name!

That day, when we had finished our business and I was about to leave my Jewish lawyer's office, she asked me an unusual question: "Do you know why it is hard for some Jewish friends of mine to believe what you call the gospel?"

My reply was very simple: "No."

The Jewish woman shared an insight into God's Word that I had never considered. Rising from her chair, she explained, "Let's go into the corporate record room. I want to show you something."

On the far wall were shelves of her clients' corporate books. She pointed to one thin book and said, "The owner is a Jew. He personally earns more than five hundred thousand dollars annually as an absentee owner with very minimal work." Then one after another she shared the workload of many of her clients, all of whom are Jews. The last set of records was for my corporations. They were long and full. Instantly, I realized that she knew something I didn't.

Her next words pierced my heart. She asked, "Do you worry and constantly pray about finances? Is your life consumed with business to the point that you now live to serve your work? Are you fulfilled by the corporations you created, or are you spending too much time and money with little return?"

At this point, I knew she had a very accurate picture of my life—maybe yours, too.

After returning to her office, we both sat down, and she looked straight into my eyes and asked, "Who planted the garden of Eden?"

To my embarrassment, I really didn't know. At the time, the Christians I attended church with quoted only from the New Testament. You see, they thought that because Jesus fulfilled the Old Testament, the promises that God had given to the Israelites were not for today. Later, however, I discovered that this was not true! All God's promises in the Old and New Testaments are for us.

Well, my lawyer reached into her drawer and pulled out the Pentateuch—the first five books in the Bible. As she read the Scriptures to me, I felt like *she* was converting *me*! A Jew converting a Christian? Yes. That day, my Jewish lawyer taught me important truths from the Old Testament that I had not known before.

She began to read from the first book:

> *And the* LORD *God planted a garden eastward in Eden; and there he put the man whom he had formed. And out of the ground made the* LORD *God to grow every tree that is pleasant to the sight, and good for food; the tree of life also in the midst of the garden, and the tree of knowledge of good and evil. And a river went out of Eden to water the garden; and from thence it was parted, and became into four heads. The name of the first is Pison: that is it which compasseth the whole land of Havilah, where there is gold; and the gold of that land is good: there is bdellium and the onyx stone. And the name of the second river is Gihon: the same is it that compasseth the whole land of Ethiopia. And the name of the third river is Hiddekel: that is it which goeth toward the east of Assyria. And the fourth river is Euphrates. And the* LORD *God took the man, and put him into the garden of Eden to dress it and to keep it.*   (Genesis 2:8–15)

Here was the answer to my lawyer's question. God Himself planted the garden of Eden, and through it, He lavished man with provisions and prosperity!

Listening intently to every word, I experienced a new insight into God's plan for man. As my lawyer read the Word of God, I thought, *Wow! In the old covenant, God revealed wisdom to the Jew to release them from financial bondage. Now, I want those promises to work in my life, too.*

Then, this Scripture immediately came to my mind: "He that walketh with wise men shall be wise: but a companion of fools shall be destroyed" (Proverbs 13:20). I was ready for a change in my life to avoid destruction. I decided right then that I would heed the wisdom.

My lawyer continued to explain that for every man, God has planted a garden designed to serve that man. The revelation struck my heart: *I have a field that God planted for me.* He planted it, watered it, and made it grow for me. In my field is all the provision I need, just as gold, bdellium, and onyx stones were provided for Adam and Eve in Eden. In fact, God created the earth to work for man, not man to work for the earth! Suddenly, my eyes were opened. I realized that my job in my God-given garden was simply to harvest it!

---

ie revelation struck my heart: *I have a field that God planted for e.* He planted it, watered it, and made it grow for me. In my field all the provision I need, just as gold, bdellium, and onyx stones ere provided for Adam and Eve in Eden. In fact, God created the rth to work for man, not man to work for the earth! Suddenly, my es were opened. I realized that my job in my God-given garden is simply to harvest it!

You see, Adam's sin brought on the curse of man working for he earth. This was not God's original intention. Adam's disobedi-nce opened the door for this curse:

And unto Adam [God] said, Because thou hast hearkened unto the voice of thy wife, and hast eaten of the tree, of which I commanded thee, saying, Thou shalt not eat of it: cursed is the ground for thy sake; in sorrow shalt thou eat of it all the days of thy life; thorns also and thistles shall it bring forth to thee;

*and thou shalt eat the herb of the field; in the sweat of thy face
shalt thou eat bread, till thou return unto the ground; for out
of it wast thou taken: for dust thou art, and unto dust shalt
thou return.*   (Genesis 3:17–19)

Suddenly, Adam's field began to produce thorns and thistles.
Now, he had to work for the land instead of it working for him.

My Jewish lawyer continued to share that many Christians tie
themselves to the curse by thinking that making a profit and being
wealthy are sinful. Finally, we ended our conversation with a little
humor. I concluded, "Well, I guess that's why the cliché isn't 'as
poor as a synagogue mouse'!"

No, the accepted norm for many people today is "as poor as a
church mouse."

GOD, WHAT IS MY FIELD?

The following week, I flew to the state of Washington. There,
I met with a manufacturer from whom my company annually
bought about $750,000 dollars of products.

At approximately 5:00 A.M., I awoke and began asking God
to show me the field He had planted for me. Instantly, the Holy
Spirit spoke to my spirit, directing me to resign as a distributor
of their materials. The instruction was explicit. I was to offer to
represent this manufacturer's products to distributors east of the
Mississippi River at a commission rate of 12 percent.

I met with the manufacturer over breakfast and shared about
finding the field God had planted for me. After I released our dis-
tributorship, the company, in turn, contracted with me to represent its products. Hallelujah, it worked! The financial pressure left
I did not need to borrow any more money for inventory. Suddenly
my warehouse, trucks, employees, all the overhead expenses, and
the associated pressures were unnecessary.

As a result of that one thought from God, I received my first commission check for $50,000 within one month! The amount of work I put in added up to less than one week, and my costs were under $1,000! I had found my field. It was working for *me*. No longer did I need to slave over my business(es) to get results. This event forever changed how I *perceived* God, which determines how I now *receive* from Him.

God has planted a field for *you*, too. In a later chapter, I will outline a practical plan to help you find your God-ordained field. Through your field, God will provide everything you need to accomplish His will for your life and achieve a sense of fulfillment. But before you find your field and start letting it work for you, you must understand a very important principle: the purpose of wealth. I must caution you that understanding the information in next chapter is critical to your success and fulfillment. Be sure to read it carefully.

2

THE PURPOSE OF
YOUR WEALTH

Many people subconsciously believe that striving for riches is wrong, yet they spend most of their waking hours laboring for paychecks. Others believe that acquiring money and wealth will bring satisfaction. However, only the peace and joy of knowing we are in God's will gives us true fulfillment.

In this chapter, we will discuss God's will regarding your prosperity, how to avoid the snare of accumulating wealth for the wrong reasons, and why this knowledge is critical to success. Now, let's examine the first of five principles that lead to a millionaire mentality: purpose.

KNOW WEALTH'S PURPOSE BEFORE YOU GET IT

You must know the purpose of something before you can adequately understand its provision or how to obtain it. In other words, knowing why you do something enables you to know *what* to do and *how* to do it. Without answering the "why" of purpose, you cannot have the "what" of provision. You see, if a person does not know why something exists, he is very likely to use it for the wrong purpose. This ultimately can turn into abuse, causing the person to lose the very thing he sought and acquired.

This is true with riches. Many people do not understand the purpose of wealth. They yield to the temptation of accumulating money for purposes other than God's original intention. At times, even Christians can do this. Many face financial conflicts without recognizing God's will. Some continually struggle with their finances and cannot free their minds of the pressure. Financial stress often leads to family breakups, health challenges, and difficulties in other areas. It breaks my heart to see this many people in financial bondage when God already has provided the answers and the means to freedom.

Well, what is the purpose of wealth, and why does God want you to have it? Deuteronomy 8:18 declares:

> But thou shalt remember the LORD thy God: for it is he that giveth thee power to get wealth, that he may establish his covenant which he sware unto thy fathers, as it is this day.

God's original purpose of wealth was to establish His covenant on earth. In the book of Genesis, the Bible explains God' covenant with Abraham (previously named Abram) for the Jews Although we will discuss this further in later chapters, notic God's promises in the following verses:

> In the same day the LORD made a covenant with Abram, saying, Unto thy seed have I given this land.
>
> (Genesis 15:18)

*And I will make of thee a great nation, and I will bless thee,
and make thy name great; and thou shalt be a blessing.*
(Genesis 12:2)

*And I will make my covenant between me and thee, and will
multiply thee exceedingly....As for me, behold, my covenant is
with thee, and thou shalt be a father of many nations.*
(Genesis 17:2, 4)

---

ne truth is that God not only has great plans for His people, but
e also provides the means to accomplish them. Yet, we struggle
lack and take His dreams to our graves. It breaks God's heart.

Ever since this covenant, the world has never considered the
ews to be a poor people.

Earlier I mentioned the idiom "as poor as a church mouse,"
ut a church mouse is not as poor as a "synagogue mouse." Why?
sn't it true that, through Jesus Christ, Christians have a better
ovenant than the Jews had? The new covenant is established upon
etter promises. What made the church believe that it was as poor
s a church mouse? Many accept the belief that the church does
ot have enough finances, and that the leftovers from a Christian's
fe are not enough to keep even a mouse alive.

Christians who believe this are grieving the Holy Spirit.
he truth is that God not only has great plans for His people,

but He also provides the means to accomplish them. Yet, we struggle in lack and take His dreams to our graves. It breaks God's heart.

You see, the work of Christ at Calvary engrafted His believers into God's covenant with Abraham. Now, we can live in limitless relationship with God. In fact, we have an exceedingly better covenant than Abraham had, because we have Christ dwelling in us through the Holy Spirit. If you are a Christian, this is true of you, too.

GOD'S COVENANT WITH YOU

To better understand God's covenant with His people and His purpose for wealth, let's study the eighth chapter of Deuteronomy. What was God's plan for the children of Israel as they wandered in the wilderness for forty years?

At God's prompting, Moses explained to the Israelites,

> All the commandments which I command thee this day shall ye observe to do, that ye may live, and multiply, and go in and possess the land which the LORD sware unto your fathers.
>
> (Deuteronomy 8:1)

Here, we see that God gave the commandments to the Israelites so that they would experience a moral, disciplined lifestyle. Obeying them would qualify them for His promises. Many times, we see the law of Moses simply as a standard by which to reveal man's sin and to control moral behavior. However, the original purpose of the commandments was to enable the Israelites to obtain God's desired blessings for them. We must understand that God did not intend for the Israelites to live in lack but instead to walk in His promises. Then we can appreciate the commandments in a new way.

Moses continued:

> *And thou shalt remember all the way which the* LORD *thy God led thee these forty years in the wilderness, to humble thee, and to prove thee, to know what was in thine heart, whether thou wouldest keep his commandments, or no.*
>
> (Deuteronomy 8:2)

It is difficult to know a man's true character until he faces stress. Pressure reveals the hidden nature. In the above verse, we learn that God decided to test the Israelites to see if they would obey Him. So He led them into a forty-year "pressure cooker." God also knew that He could determine if they were wise by correcting them, because a wise person benefits from correction and reproof. Yet, a fool turns against authority.

---

ere is a reason why some Christians do not yet have God's ovision. It is because they have not yet proven that they will hear d obey God in living by His every word.

> *A reproof entereth more into a wise man than an hundred stripes into a fool.*   (Proverbs 17:10)

> *A fool despiseth his father's instruction: but he that regardeth reproof is prudent.*   (Proverbs 15:5)

Now, God walked throughout the trial with the Israelites:

> *And he humbled thee, and suffered thee to hunger, and fed thee with manna, which thou knewest not, neither did thy fathers know; that he might make thee know that man doth not live by bread only, but by every word that proceedeth out of the mouth of the LORD doth man live.*   (Deuteronomy 8:3)

God wanted the nation of Israel to live on the sustaining revelation of His Word, not on the provision they could earn with their own hands. Thus, He desired that they become revelation-oriented, not provision-oriented.

God tested the Israelites for forty years, so they would learn that man does not live by bread alone but by every word from God. You see, provision comes from God's voice. However, the Israelites did not expect their supply from their heavenly Father's voice. In fact, they did not even want to hear from Him! Think of it: The Israelites spent forty years in the wilderness, because they would not hear and obey God! Thus, they could not walk in His promises.

Now, because of the finished work of Jesus Christ, the church has far better promises than Israel ever had. Yes, God tested the Israelites for a season to prove whether they would obey Him before He released the provision. And God's nature does no change. The way the Lord communicated and tested His people i the Old Testament is the same as He tests us today. "*Jesus Chri. [is] the same yesterday, and to day, and for ever*" (Hebrews 13:8 Israel learned to become an obedient people in an unfriendly lanc Jesus also learned obedience through suffering in a hostile env ronment. Similarly, the early church learned to obey God in a antagonistic setting. Therefore, it is highly likely that we will fac hostile circumstances to motivate us to obey God's Word, too. Jesus had to learn obedience through suffering, it is certain th we will, as well. (See John 15:20.) There is a reason why son Christians do not yet have God's provision. It is because they ha not yet proven that they will hear and obey God in living by F every word.

You may be thinking, *I thought this book was about the millionaire mentality—how to get money.* It is, but you need to do it according to God's plan, not the flesh's way. There is a big difference. You can get money for the wrong reasons both illegally and legally. However, these ungodly motivations will not produce blessings in your life. You see, I am not writing simply about money but about its connection with God's purpose. This is about what He desires for you, to form you so that you will be trustworthy with whatever He puts into your hands. Otherwise, any wealth you accumulate will be a curse to you.

Now, when you begin to accumulate wealth and blessings God's way, it is critical that you remember where it came from:

> For the LORD thy God bringeth thee into a good land, a land of brooks of water, of fountains and depths that spring out of valleys and hills; a land of wheat, and barley, and vines, and fig trees, and pomegranates; a land of oil olive, and honey; a land wherein thou shalt eat bread without scarceness, thou shalt not lack any thing in it; a land whose stones are iron, and out of whose hills thou mayest dig brass. When thou hast eaten and art full, then thou shalt bless the LORD thy God for the good land which he hath given thee. Beware that thou forget not the LORD thy God, in not keeping his commandments, and his judgments, and his statutes, which I command thee this day: lest when thou hast eaten and art full, and hast built goodly houses, and dwelt therein; and when thy herds and thy flocks multiply, and thy silver and thy gold is multiplied, and all that thou hast is multiplied; then thine heart be lifted up, and thou forget the LORD thy God, which brought thee forth out of the land of Egypt, from the house of bondage; who led thee through that great and terrible wilderness, wherein were fiery serpents, and scorpions, and drought, where there was no water; who brought thee forth water out of the rock of flint; who fed thee in the wilderness with manna, which thy fathers

> *knew not, that he might humble thee, and that he might prove thee, to do thee good at thy latter end; and thou say in thine heart, My power and the might of mine hand hath gotten me this wealth.*   (Deuteronomy 8:7–17)

God's design is to teach you to excel, prosper, and profit with wave of prosperity crashing in your life.

Remember, God tested the children of Israel so that He could bless them in the end. However, when the blessings came, God did not want the Israelites to become slack in trusting and obeying Him.

I have watched many people cross the threshold into prosperity. Beforehand, they had correctly tithed and given offerings. Their declarations, actions, and motivations had been consistent with God's Word. Then, creative ideas started to flow. Financial increase came, and the power of God's anointing infiltrated their hearts and lives. However, at that point, they began to think the fruit of their cultivation and development was enough to sustain them. They forgot God. Then, many kinds of difficulties and negative situations afflicted them. I have found that it is better to prove to God that we will trust and obey Him before we obtain His blessings; otherwise, blessings may become our downfall.

Let's read the next two verses after Deuteronomy 8:18:

But thou shalt remember the LORD thy God: for it is he that giveth thee power to get wealth, that he may establish his covenant which he sware unto thy fathers, as it is this day. And it shall be, if thou do at all forget the LORD thy God, and walk after other gods, and serve them, and worship them, I testify against you this day that ye shall surely perish. As the nations which the LORD destroyeth before your face, so shall ye perish; because ye would not be obedient unto the voice of the LORD your God. (Deuteronomy 8:18–20)

God wants you to be in the flow of money. However, if you forget Him and His purpose for wealth, then you may lose it as quickly as you obtained it.

We have learned from Deuteronomy that God would not give the Promised Land to the nation of Israel until the people obeyed Him. Today, when I find a group of people not walking in the provision of God's vision, I know there is a reason for it. This may sound harsh, but the truth is that they may not yet be trustworthy. They may not have passed the test of obedience in some area of their lives. Now, these people may have good intentions, but you know the adage "The road to hell is paved with good intentions." Good intentions do not merit God's blessings. To obtain prosperous results, you must have fellowship with God and obey Him.

Let's read the Amplified version of a passage in Isaiah:

Thus says the Lord, your Redeemer, the Holy One of Israel: I am the Lord your God, Who teaches you to profit, Who leads you in the way that you should go. Oh, that you had hearkened to My commandments! Then your peace and prosperity would have been like a flowing river; and your righteousness [the holiness and purity of the nation] like the [abundant] waves of the sea. Your offspring would have been like the sand, and your descendants like the offspring of the sea; their name would not be cut off or destroyed from before Me.

(Isaiah 48:17–19 AMP)

In effect, God said to the Israelites, "If only you had listened to Me and followed Me, you would have experienced a constant flow of prosperity in your lives. Instead, look at what you reaped. I would have perpetuated blessings through your children, but now it must cease." Then Israel returned to bondage.

God's design is to teach you to excel, prosper, and profit with waves of prosperity crashing in your life. Should a still pond satisfy you? No! Believe and expect God to release torrents of blessing and prosperity in your direction!

Do you realize that there is more money on this earth than people know what to do with? Yet how many of us think we don't have enough? The problem is in our perspective. It's time to change our thinking about money.

FOLLOW GOD'S PLAN OF WEALTH

One day, God spoke to me saying that it was my time for supernatural increase. After, I had an opportunity to buy stock which was selling at or about thirty cents per share. However, fear gripped me, and I did not buy it, and within a matter of days, the closing price on this stock was $2.90 per share! Now, believe me, I am not advocating buying stock. However, I now realize that because I did not listen to God's voice, I lost my opportunity to profit.

How can you reclaim lost opportunity? You cannot. The generations of Israelites who died in the wilderness did not receive their portion of God's promises. It is simple: When you do not follow the Lord's directions, you lose His blessings. This is heart rending, but God does not guarantee unconditional blessings. He guarantees only unconditional love. In other words, God will love you regardless of whether or not you choose to serve Him and receive blessings!

Some might say that God's a God of second chances. This is a nice statement but not a guarantee. When I read my Bible, I see that many people did not receive second chances. In fact, some disobeyed and died the next day! Not everyone automatically has a second, third, or fourth chance with God. When this does happen, we should thank God for His grace, but not plan our lives around it. It is far better to obey God when He speaks than to fail Him repeatedly like Israel did. Following God's purpose the first time is how to pass His tests.

Ask yourself, Am I in a time of testing to prove if I will live by every word that proceeds from the mouth of God? Do I believe that my sustenance will come through God's promises if I am obedient to Him? Will He trust me with what He will put into my hands? These are critical issues to resolve. It does not matter whether you are a new babe in Christ; a very mature, Bible-quoting believer; somewhere between these; or not a Christian at all. God wants to see if He can trust you. The Bible promises us that *"all these blessings shall come on thee, and overtake thee, if thou shalt hearken unto the voice of the LORD thy God"* (Deuteronomy 28:2).

Deception can cause anyone to think he is right with God. However, if God's blessings are not overtaking him, something is wrong. I have heard it said, "God will never advance you beyond your last act of disobedience." Do you feel stuck in lack and unfulfillment? Be honest with yourself as you check your heart. Ask the Lord to reveal any areas of disobedience in your life or areas in which you do not completely trust Him.

GOD DESIRES TO PROSPER HIS PEOPLE

God's intent has never been for His people to lack. Throughout His Word, we find this to be true. The Bible promises:

> *And all these blessings shall come on thee, and overtake thee, if thou shalt hearken unto the voice of the* LORD *thy God.*
>
> (Deuteronomy 28:2)

> *O taste and see that the* LORD *is good: blessed is the man that trusteth in him. O fear the* LORD, *ye his saints: for there is no want to them that fear him. The young lions do lack, and suffer hunger: but they that seek the* LORD *shall not want any good thing.*
>
> (Psalm 34:8–10)

> *Let them shout for joy, and be glad, that favour my righteous cause: yea, let them say continually, Let the* LORD *be magnified, which hath pleasure in the prosperity of his servant.*
>
> (Psalm 35:27)

God kept the Israelites in the desert for forty years so that t[hey] would learn that man does not live by bread alone but by ev[ery] word that proceeds from the mouth of God. Yet man's menta[lity] hasn't changed; we still believe that we have to work for a liv[ing]. Therefore, we spend only a little time, if any time at all, with Go[d to] hear from Him.

Here, the Bible says to magnify the Lord, who takes pleasu[re] in my prosperity. I would much rather make God happy by bles[s]ing and prospering me than upset Him by being needy and wa[nt]ing! What about you?

Remember, Proverbs 10:22 says, "*The blessing of the LORD, it maketh rich, and he addeth no sorrow with it.*"

Do you wake up every morning shouting for joy because of God's provision, or do you speak from a sorrowful motivation? "I can't imagine where the money will come from. Another day, another dollar. It's murky Monday, tribulation Tuesday, what's-it-all-worth Wednesday, thankless Thursday, or frazzled Friday. It will be a miracle if I get through the week. That miserable paycheck I get is never enough money to do anything with. Everyone—the government, my family, and even God—wants to get hold of it. Everybody has a hand in my pocket."

Do you feel that the money you earn each week is not fulfilling your dreams for tomorrow? Have you already spent this month's paycheck and still have to pay the bills? Paying off yesterday's expenses is not an exciting motivation for work. Don't defeat yourself. Let God's Word revive your spirit. Here's what He has to say about your situation:

For the LORD God is a sun and shield: the LORD will give grace and glory: no good thing will he withhold from them that walk uprightly. (Psalm 84:11)

For evildoers shall be cut off: but those that wait upon the LORD, they shall inherit the earth....A little that a righteous man hath is better than the riches of many wicked....I have been young, and now am old; yet have I not seen the righteous forsaken, nor his seed begging bread. (Psalm 37:9, 16, 25)

Praise ye the LORD. Blessed is the man that feareth the LORD, that delighteth greatly in his commandments. His seed shall be mighty upon earth: the generation of the upright shall be blessed. Wealth and riches shall be in his house: and his righteousness endureth for ever. (Psalm 112:1–3)

Honour the LORD with thy substance, and with the firstfruits of all thine increase: so shall thy barns be filled with plenty, and thy presses shall burst out with new wine.

(Proverbs 3:9–10)

Humility is the fear of the LORD; its wages are riches and honor and life. (Proverbs 22:4 NIV)

If you are willing and obedient, you will eat the good things of the land. (Isaiah 1:19 NIV)

They will rebuild the ancient ruins and restore the places long devastated; they will renew the ruined cities that have been devastated for generations. Strangers will shepherd your flocks; foreigners will work your fields and vineyards. And you will be called priests of the LORD, you will be named ministers of our God. You will feed on the wealth of nations, and in their riches you will boast. (Isaiah 61:4–6 NIV)

These Scriptures are only a small sampling of biblical evidenc that God desires to bless you financially. Read all sixty-six book of the Bible, and note every verse that deals with finances, includ ing work, income, wealth, riches, deceitfulness of riches, owne ship, stewardship, and other related topics. If you do this, you wi find more on this subject than any other topic in the entire Wor of God. Do you know why? It is because your finances can inflt ence you as much as God does.

Jesus said:

No one can serve two masters. Either you will hate the one and love the other, or you will be devoted to the one and despise the other. You cannot serve both God and money.

(Matthew 6:24 NIV)

God knows how people think. They will invest forty to sixty hours a week to work and earn money yet complain about their pastor's Sunday message if it lasts more than forty-five minutes. Here is an interesting thought: What would happen if we reversed the cycle? What if people spent forty hours a week in the Word and one hour working to get all the money they need? God kept the Israelites in the desert for forty years so that they would learn that man does not live by bread alone but by every word that proceeds from the mouth of God. Yet man's mentality hasn't changed; we still believe that we have to work for a living. Therefore, we spend only a little time, if any time at all, with God to hear from Him.

Who will we serve? The choice is ours. Will we live in cursed or blessed environments? I made my own choice early. I decided it was worth spending more time in the Word than trying to make money. Not surprisingly, I discovered that there is more money in the Word than in making money! How did I get it? I learned that it comes from reading and meditating on the Bible and spending time with God. He gives creative ideas to me that generate more income than I could do "beating the bushes" in business on my own.

Listening to the voice of the Lord will release you from the stress of continually thinking about money and how to get or keep it. God will pour so many inspired ideas and blessings into you that you will not be able to contain them all. In His Word, He declares:

> I love those who love me, and those who seek me diligently will find me. Riches and honor are with me, enduring riches and righteousness. My fruit is better than gold, yes, than fine gold, and my revenue than choice silver. I traverse the way of righteousness, in the midst of the paths of justice, that I may cause those who love me to inherit wealth, that I may fill their treasuries.
> (Proverbs 8:17–21 NKJV)

Does this mean that God has no interest in money? No. Remember, He owns it all. He simply desires for you to use it properly. Think about it: God loves those who love Him and seek Him. He causes them to inherit wealth and have full treasuries!

While this book is about the millionaire mentality, it does not necessarily promise that by reading it, your balance sheet will show a net worth of millions of dollars. Actually, your mind-set should be influenced by the knowledge that your worth is far greater than any amount of money.

You see, only when you comprehend the exorbitant price that God paid for you can you fully appreciate your dignity and personal value to Him. We know that the price someone is willing to pay for an item determines its true value. Your value to God is set. He already determined it by His awesome sacrifice of His only begotten Son!

Never underestimate what God wants to do with your life. Recognize that His Word declares:

> Beloved, I wish above all things that thou mayest prosper and
> be in health, even as thy soul prospereth.   (3 John 1:2)

> Now unto him that is able to do exceeding abundantly above
> all that we ask or think, according to the power that worketh
> in us, unto him be glory.   (Ephesians 3:20–21)

I pray that God will open the eyes of your understanding and cause you to see the entire financial and material arena from His viewpoint. Remember, how you perceive God is how you will receive from God!

Let's close this chapter with a prayer for understanding the purpose of wealth:

Heavenly Father,

Thank You for establishing a holy covenant with me through Your Son, Jesus. I believe, according to Your Word, that You desire to bless and prosper me, and will cause me to fulfill Your heavenly dream for my life.

When Your blessings come upon me, O Lord, help me not to forget You. Let me keep my eyes focused on You, Father, and not on wealth and prosperity. Help me to be a good steward of Your blessings. In Jesus' name, amen.

3

FIND THE FIELD GOD PLANTED FOR YOU

Never forget that how you perceive God determines how you receive from God. You are very important to Your heavenly Father. He has a vision for His kingdom, and you have a vital role to play in His dream. To help you in that role, He has prepared a place of provision for you. Locating it will free your time, so you can devote more effort and finances to His work instead of spending all your time working to earn a living. The key to getting there is finding that field. In this chapter, I will show you how to do that, as we explore the second of the five principles that lead to the millionaire mentality: prophetic vision. Then, in the following chapter, we will dive into more detail about prophetic vision, specifically how to activate your dreams.

JUST ONE WORD FROM GOD

In 1983, my wife and I sold our businesses; then, in 1984, we began a church in our home with only three people. After a few months, I asked God why He had taken the gift of giving away from me, for many years before this, God had blessed us so we could substantially support His kingdom's work both in the United States and abroad. Now, our income was significantly less.

The instant the words left my mouth, the Holy Spirit spoke to my spirit. "I have not taken the gift of giving from you," He said. "You have taken it from Me!"

I walked outside and asked, "Lord, where is the field You planted for me?"

Immediately the Spirit of the Lord spoke to me again. This time, He told me to buy my neighbors' house for thirty thousand dollars. I realized that its market value was at least seventy-five thousand dollars. However, I obediently walked to my neighbors home and shared the revelation about God's field with the owners They immediately replied that the house was worth at least seventy-five thousand dollars and was not for sale! After a little discussion, I left, saying, "When you are ready to sell it to me, just call."

Within three months, I received that call, and my neighbor sold their home to me for only thirty thousand. After a ten thousand dollar cosmetic face-lift, I sold the house in the same year for ninety-seven thousand. Just one thought from God produced fifty-seven thousand dollar gross profit.

I now maintain a perspective that God always has a field planted for me, which is ready to harvest. All I must do is see Him to find it and reap it.

HARVEST THE FIELD OF YOUR DREAMS

I believe that the following verses apply to any field that God has planted for His children, whether it is preaching the gospel to unbelievers, ministering, teaching, working in business, and so forth.

> Jesus saith unto them, My meat is to do the will of him that sent me, and to finish his work. Say not ye, There are yet four months, and then cometh harvest? behold, I say unto you, Lift up your eyes, and look on the fields; for they are white already to harvest. And he that reapeth receiveth wages, and gathereth fruit unto life eternal: that both he that soweth and he that reapeth may rejoice together. And herein is that saying true, One soweth, and another reapeth. I sent you to reap that whereon ye bestowed no labour: other men laboured, and ye are entered into their labours.   (John 4:34–38)

As we continue our journey deeper into the millionaire mentality, get ready to see *your* field white and ready for harvest before your eyes. Now, I encourage you to carefully examine your life as we answer the following important questions:

+ What is a cursed field?

+ What is my attitude regarding my financial future?

+ Where is the field that God has planted for me?

For a very thorough and informative teaching about finding the specific field God planted for you, please refer to my eight-tape series: "True Success—How to Find the Field God Has Planted for You," available on audio, video, or CD. Subjects include understanding the symptoms of a cursed field, how to escape the field of curse, identifying the origins of your work environment, recognizing your giftings versus your adaptations based upon financial need, coming out of need into God's purposes, and much more.

BIBLICAL IDENTIFICATIONS OF A CURSED FIELD

Maybe you have a vision, but for years something has held you back, preventing you from marching toward its fulfillment. If you have felt a strangling or stifling of your dream, perhaps there is a curse in your life. Before proceeding, you must close all the open doors for curses.[1]

Answering the following questions will help you to determine if you have a cursed field. Be brutally honest with yourself as you answer these questions.

1. In your current employment, do you set your own income level and the direction of your vocation, or does someone else determine your worth?

2. Do you thoroughly enjoy what you do, or is it only a means to get money?

3. Is the work of your hands like the curse God gave to Adam, as we read earlier? (See Genesis 3:17–19.)

4. In Deuteronomy 28, we can read about the blessings and curses of the Law. People who violated that Law encountered problems and economic depravity. Have you ever encountered any of the following curses?

But it shall come to pass, if thou wilt not hearken unto the voice of the LORD thy God, to observe to do all his commandments and his statutes which I command thee this day; that all these curses shall come upon thee, and overtake thee: cursed shalt thou be in the city, and cursed shalt thou be in the field. Cursed shall be thy basket and thy store.

(Deuteronomy 28:15–17)

Thou shalt plant a vineyard, and shalt not gather the grapes thereof. Thine ox shall be slain before thine eyes, and thou shalt not eat thereof: thine ass shall be violently taken away

---

1. For practical strategies regarding breaking curses, please refer to my book *How to Identify and Remove Curses*, which is also available on tape. To discover more about how the fall in the garden of Eden produced a curse on mankind, how to break free from this curse, and how to help set others free in Jesus' name, refer m book *Conquering Your Unseen Enemies: How Jesus Sets You Free.*

from before thy face, and shall not be restored to thee: thy sheep shall be given unto thine enemies, and thou shalt have none to rescue them.…The fruit of thy land, and all thy labours, shall a nation which thou knowest not eat up; and thou shalt be only oppressed and crushed alway.

(Deuteronomy 28:30–31, 33)

Thou shalt carry much seed out into the field, and shalt gather but little in; for the locust shall consume it. Thou shalt plant vineyards, and dress them, but shalt neither drink of the wine, nor gather the grapes; for the worms shall eat them. Thou shalt have olive trees throughout all thy coasts, but thou shalt not anoint thyself with the oil; for thine olive shall cast his fruit. Thou shalt beget sons and daughters, but thou shalt not enjoy them; for they shall go into captivity. All thy trees and fruit of thy land shall the locust consume.…He shall lend to thee, and thou shalt not lend to him: he shall be the head, and thou shalt be the tail.…Therefore shalt thou serve thine enemies which the LORD shall send against thee, in hunger, and in thirst, and in nakedness, and in want of all things: and he shall put a yoke of iron upon thy neck, until he have destroyed thee.

(Deuteronomy 28:38–42, 44, 48)

YOUR ATTITUDE DETERMINES YOUR ALTITUDE

Now is the time to change! You must correct your views about our job and income. This is an important part of finding your ield to harvest.

During my divorce and remarriage to Faye in 1975, I complained about my work and how poor my pay was. Then, one day, read the following verse in the Bible:

> *And whatsoever ye do in word or deed, do all in the name of the Lord Jesus, giving thanks to God and the Father by him.*
> (Colossians 3:17)

This Scripture revealed a big problem in my life. For years, many of my friends and I continually complained about our jobs. I realized that I had never worked *in Jesus' name*. From that moment on, I performed every task, every weld on each car, proclaiming, "In Jesus' name." Many times for weeks, I repeated over my work, "In Jesus' name." Then, one day, I noticed that my sense of work had changed, because I was continually giving thanks to God. Wow, what a change it was! After a while, I grew to love my job, it even became a joy, yet nothing had changed except my attitude.

One of the greatest fallacies is that circumstances must change for joy to come. No! Right where you are, begin to conform your thinking, words, and actions to the Word of God. Then joy will follow!

> *In every thing give thanks: for this is the will of God in Christ Jesus concerning you.*   (1 Thessalonians 5:18)

When you change your attitude, you change your altitude. Also remember that "*death and life are in the power of the tongue and they that love it shall eat the fruit thereof*" (Proverbs 18:21).

Now you are on your way to washing your mentality by th Word, so God can show you His will for your life.

> *And be not conformed to this world: but be ye transformed by the renewing of your mind, that ye may prove what is that good, and acceptable, and perfect, will of God.*
> (Romans 12:2)

Renewing your mind with God's truth brings you into H will. How can you do this? You renew your mind by washing with the Word of God, which means reading the Bible and meditating on it, and asking God how to apply it to your life.

> *Christ also loved the church, and gave himself for it; that he might sanctify and cleanse it with the washing of water by the word, that he might present it to himself a glorious church, not having spot, or wrinkle, or any such thing; but that it should be holy and without blemish.*   (Ephesians 5:25–27)

HOW TO IDENTIFY THE FIELD GOD PLANTED FOR YOU

It is God's will for you to work and harvest the field of your dreams, which He planted for you to enjoy. To determine whether you have discovered God's field for you, answer these questions:

1. Do God's blessings in Deuteronomy 28 describe your life and work?

> *And it shall come to pass, if thou shalt hearken diligently unto the voice of the LORD thy God, to observe and to do all his commandments which I command thee this day, that the LORD thy God will set thee on high above all nations of the earth: and all these blessings shall come on thee, and overtake thee, if thou shalt hearken unto the voice of the LORD thy God. Blessed shalt thou be in the city, and blessed shalt thou be in the field. Blessed shall be the fruit of thy body, and the fruit of thy ground, and the fruit of thy cattle, the increase of thy kine, and the flocks of thy sheep. Blessed shall be thy basket and thy store. Blessed shalt thou be when thou comest in, and blessed shalt thou be when thou goest out. The LORD shall cause thine enemies that rise up against thee to be smitten before thy face: they shall come out against thee one way, and flee before thee seven ways. The LORD shall command the blessing upon thee in thy storehouses, and in all that thou settest thine hand unto; and he shall bless thee in the land*

which the Lord *thy God giveth thee.*

(Deuteronomy 28:1–8)

And the Lord *shall make thee plenteous in goods, in the fruit
of thy body, and in the fruit of thy cattle, and in the fruit of thy
ground, in the land which the* Lord *sware unto thy fathers to
give thee. The* Lord *shall open unto thee his good treasure, the
heaven to give the rain unto thy land in his season, and to bless
all the work of thine hand: and thou shalt lend unto many
nations, and thou shalt not borrow. And the* Lord *shall make
thee the head, and not the tail; and thou shalt be above only, and
thou shalt not be beneath; if that thou hearken unto the commandments of the* Lord *thy God, which I command thee this
day, to observe and to do them: And thou shalt not go aside from
any of the words which I command thee this day, to the right
hand, or to the left, to go after other gods to serve them.*

(Deuteronomy 28:11–14)

2. Simply consider the most fulfilling work you could do. Is
that what you do now?

3. Are you daily in your element? Are you blossoming and
using your giftings?

4. Do you feel that your daily tasks have lasting significance, o
does every day bring a sense of never-ending drudgery?

5. At the end of the day, do you sense growth in your persona
life's dream?

Right now, maybe you are thinking, *I am not experiencing any
thing from the abundant field that God has planted for me.* Don't giv
up. It is out there for you and will fit you like a glove. You may war
to begin working toward your dreams on a part-time basis. Allo
them to grow until you are fully experiencing them! In everythin
you do, always remember that your attitude, words, and actior
affect your future!

Remember, if you obey God, all His blessings and promises are yours. No man can stop what God has declared for you. Your heavenly Father wants to overtake you with His blessings so that your latter days will outshine your former. If you obey Him, He will bless you.

If you are not yet experiencing the blessings, there is a reason. Understand that there is a cause for everything. In the Bible, this principle of cause and effect is called *"seedtime and harvest"* (Genesis 8:22). If you can root out the cause of your lack, then release that which God originally intended for you (blessings, wealth, fulfillment, and prosperity in every area of your life), then you can enjoy the effects.

---

member, if you obey God, all His blessings and promises are urs. No man can stop what God has declared for you.

You see, in writing to the Galatians, the apostle Paul said,

Christ hath redeemed us from the curse of the law, being made a curse for us: for it is written, Cursed is every one that hangeth on a tree: that the blessing of Abraham might come on the Gentiles through Jesus Christ; that we might receive the promise of the Spirit through faith. (Galatians 3:13–14)

Having the blessing of Abraham means that, first, you will receive the promise of the Spirit through faith, the full person of the Spirit of God flowing in your life. Second, having the blessing of Abraham also means that you will have everything God promised Abraham in His covenant. Therefore, you have the right to receive God's blessings coming and going, and every enemy that rises against you will be smitten before your face and dispersed, according to Deuteronomy 28. Are you experiencing these promises? If not, you can! Keep reading. Prepare yourself for the next chapter, where we will launch further into the principle of prophetic vision.

4

ACTIVATE YOUR DREAM SEEDS

Continuing in the millionaire mentality principle of prophetic vision, let me assure you that you have everything at your disposal to accomplish your dreams. Why, then, are the graveyards of the world filled with aborted dreams? It need not be this way. In this chapter, you will learn how to plant your dream seeds, so that they will mature fully as God originally intended.

Today, many people have dreams in their spirits that have not yet been activated. Is this your situation? Have everyday events and challenges obscured your dream? Do you face circumstances that cause you to limit, bind, and restrain your vision? Perhaps you have attempted to accomplish your dream but were unsuccessful. Don't give into the enemy's temptation to shove your visions aside in frustration and say, "Forget it! This is too involved!" This is *not* God's plan for you.

MAN IS TO RULE

What then *is* God's intention for your life? To discover the answer to this question, let's examine God's original dream for Adam and Eve.

> *So God created man in his own image, in the image of God created he him; male and female created he them. And God blessed them, and God said unto them, Be fruitful, and multiply, and replenish the earth, and subdue it: and have dominion over the fish of the sea, and over the fowl of the air, and over every living thing that moveth upon the earth.* (Genesis 1:27–28)

What an awesome responsibility this was! Think about what God dreamed for the first man and woman. In effect, He commanded them, saying, "I want you to start being fruitful. Multiply. Wherever you find loss in the earth, replenish it. Remake the entire earth, and subdue anything that is lawless. When you finish all this and the earth is the way it needs to be, I want you to rule over it. This is My dream for you. Everything I have created is under your influence. Adam, I invest within you the full authority and capacity to administer creation."

What did Adam do in response to God's dream? He gave direction to the animals and named them. He imparted purpose to everything in existence. How did Adam do this? He operated his dream with a divine purpose and identity. You see, his identity was not in his humanity but born of God's original intention for mankind.

Actually, God destined *all* mankind to rule, control, and take absolute dominion over His environment. We can see this in Psalm 8:4–6, which reveals our heavenly Father's thoughts of man:

> *What is man, that thou art mindful of him? and the son of man, that thou visitest him? For thou hast made him a little lower than the angels, and hast crowned him with glory and*

honour. Thou madest him to have dominion over the works of thy hands; thou hast put all things under his feet.

---

believe that God has so glorified us that it is the earth's privilege
or us to walk on it. It is the air's privilege for us to breathe it. We are
ot debtors to oxygen, but oxygen is a debtor to us. I don't believe
e owe money anything. However, money owes us everything,
ecause money exists only for our use.

Here, we see that God created man in His image and bestowed
glory and honor upon him. Have you ever felt dishonored because
of other people's actions, attitudes, or motivations toward you?
Please realize that this does not diminish God's thoughts about
you. Change your thinking to conform to God's thoughts and His
Word.

You and I carry God's glory and honor within us. We are His
children! I believe that God has so glorified us that it is the earth's
privilege for us to walk on it. It is the air's privilege for us to breathe
t. We are not debtors to oxygen, but oxygen is a debtor to us. I
don't believe we owe money anything. However, money owes us
everything, because money exists only for our use. Think about it.
We are the purpose of money's existence. God has created you and
me with glory, honor, and dignity. We live in the realm of domin-
on—designed to rule, not to be subject to others.

For example, consider a child's development. A baby knows only how to act humanly. Having recently come from God, he longs to express his freedom. Therefore, he screams loudly until he gets his own way. You see, he knows only that he has come to the earth to rule and be served. Adults then tell him, "No, no, that's not how it is in the real world." They condition him to become a servant of his environment and its systems and regulations, which, in turn, squash his entire motivation to create. Later, people might wonder why he lacks motivation. One reason is that when he was developing the ability to stand up and rule an environment, adults shut him up, sat him down, and told him that he was wrong. Instead, what would have resulted if they had directed the child's motivation into the creative avenues of God?

Some actions that we interpret as rebellion in children really are not that at all. They simply are expressions of a spirit that does not want others to contain and restrain it. I believe one of the greatest hindrances to success is the educational process to which we subject our children. Are secular schools training them to live according to what God has promised them? Are we teaching them to run this world because they have all God's blessings? The vast majority of children would answer these questions with "No." We don't educate them to rule, reign, and take dominion. Instead, we teach them to subject themselves to a ruling, conforming society which dictates what they can do. As adults, then, they become disciplined with bondage, restrictions, and limitations instead of the limitless ability to rule.

Most of the psychology by which we live is not biblically sound. It steals the very roots and elements of our godly dignity in creation. It takes away the original intention to rule and take dominion in the earth. I believe our environment has so affected us that feels illegal to think beyond the boundaries of our limitations. We are uncertain whether God wants us to explore uncharted realms. However, the truth is that God says we can do all things when we represent and obey Him on the earth.

After this brief study of God's original intention for humanity, we see that He programmed *every* man, woman, and child to rule. This includes you! Never forget that your heavenly Father has programmed you this way, as He did Adam and Eve. God designed you to rule; does this mean He created you to have this type of influence? Oh, yes, He did. He has provided you everything you need to bear fruit, multiply, replenish, subdue, and take dominion. You see, God's plan through Jesus Christ is to redeem you from your limitations and invite you into His limitless life, so you can rule in this earth. Before He made you, God envisioned your purpose within His being and created you with the abilities to achieve that purpose.

Now, you need to tap into and release those abilities to operate. It's time to identify what will stimulate the dream that God has already sown in your spirit. What will move you to action? By realizing this:

+ You are the product of God's dream before creation.

+ God designed all creation to provide you with an opportunity to exercise your abilities and achieve His dreams within you.

Now, you must activate your dreams, instead of allowing them to lie dormant. Don't live as others do. God designed you to be different from the average person. How, then, shall you live?

MAN IS TO REAP PERPETUAL HARVESTS

As we read in Genesis 1:28, God's original design for man was to bear fruit, multiply, replenish, subdue, and dominate. Let's examine each of these aspects we are to fulfill.

BEAR FRUIT

Being fruitful implies enjoying perpetual harvests. You see, my definition of *fruitful* is the process of bringing seeds to maturity, gathering the harvest, and producing more seeds from the harvest to create perpetual harvests. Fruitfulness does not merely mean that something bears fruit. Yes, there may be fruit, but true fruitfulness is when the fruit bears seed, which creates new fruit, and then the new fruit creates new seeds, and so on. It is a perpetuation, a continuum, not an end in itself.

MULTIPLY

My definition of *multiply* is to increase something by duplicating. God designed us to duplicate. Consider business. Many businesses do not originate with entirely original ideas. For example, Christopher Columbus' radical idea of the world being round was not really new; he stated that his thought was inspired from reading God's Word![2]

You see, everything is a pattern of something else. This is why franchising does so well in the United States. Coca-Cola, Pepsi and McDonald's are now worldwide. Why? They multiplied. Which people make a lot of money? Multipliers!

REPLENISH

Replenish means to constantly supply refills to whatever becomes depleted. Instead of complaining about what is empty, God designed us to bring fullness to our world. We dislike areas of vacuum in society, such as challenges with people groups. Well, God designed us to fix these problems. We are the answer to everything depleted in life.

Have you seen an area of depletion that bothers you? For instance, does the decay of a nearby city block grieve you? Does the demise of our nation's morals and values concern you? Do

2. Gary DeMar, *God and Government: A Biblical and Historical Study*, vol. 1 (Georgia: American Vision Press, 2001), 126.
For more information about this and similar stories, refer to my book *It Only Takes One*.

your heart break when you hear about abused or abandoned children or aborted babies? Does the loneliness of an elderly neighbor tug at your heart? Do you have compassion for a young mother down the street who is dying of cancer?

---

od created you to fill the emptiness and to fix the brokenness, restore all things to their full capacity according to His original ention and purpose. God created you to make a difference.

You must understand why you are here. God has put His children—including you and me—on this earth to replenish city blocks; to stand for His values; to save abused and abandoned children, and to keep abortion from happening; to love the elderly; to pray for the sick; and to meet the needs of this world. You are not here to complain about the problems. No; God created you to fill the emptiness and to fix the brokenness, to restore all things to their full capacity according to His original intention and purpose. God created you to make a difference. The world needs you to fill its gaps and to mend its broken walls. I have heard it said, "Find a need and fill it." Indeed, that's mankind's job.

SUBDUE

How do you *subdue*? By bringing all chaotic, lawless, aimless obstacles into subjection to your purpose. God gave you the gift of subduing. Therefore, you can conquer anything in His name.

> *Nay, in all these things we are more than conquerors through him that loved us.*   (Romans 8:37)

> *But Jesus beheld them, and said unto them, With men this is impossible; but with God all things are possible.*
> (Matthew 19:26)

Recently, I met the manager of an engineering group, which works for a large conglomerate of oil companies. Surprisingly, this manager is not an engineer himself. In fact, he did not even graduate from junior college. Yet, his annual salary is $125,000! I asked how he could manage engineers without knowing what they do.

He replied, "I wouldn't want to waste my time. I don't have to understand what they do. I just need to get them to do what I tell them, and make sure they know how to do it."

"Who gives your orders?" I asked.

"Someone who also doesn't know what they do!" he answered

I realized that he was right. The manager's supervisor also had no idea how these systems worked. His educational background was not engineering, either. He simply had the subduing responsibility of bringing these people under purpose and making sure they carried out his orders.

At this point, you may be thinking, *Why am I reading all this? I thought I was about to learn how to have a millionaire mentality.* Well, this is the root of it. Much of the millionaire mentality is recognizing that God designed you to bear fruit, multiply, replenish, subdue, and dominate. When you understand this, you will be ready to plant your dream seeds in fertile soil.

DOMINATE

Lastly, God made you to have *dominion*, that is, to rule absolutely. However, sometimes you may feel like retreating from are of challenge, because you feel ill-equipped to influence the circumstances. Allow your faith to play an important role here. No matter how you feel, place your faith and trust in God, knowing that He designed you to influence *every* environment you encounter. Remember, His Word declares this, so it must be true.

GOD IS OUR SOURCE OF WEALTH

From the beginning, God intended to be our source of wealth. Please don't misunderstand this. There is nothing wrong with working and earning an income, but it should not be all the revenue you receive. After all, God *does* say that we must provide for our families:

> But if any provide not for his own, and specially for those of his own house, he hath denied the faith, and is worse than an infidel.   (1 Timothy 5:8)

However, since God—not your job—is your source, don't limit your income to your job. God has other avenues through which He desires to prosper you. Yet, they *all* come from Him.

Suppose you say to your supervisor at work one day, "I want to read Deuteronomy 28:1–14 to you. I expect that all the blessings listed here will come from this corporation." Before you finish reading, however, your manager docks your pay, because he thinks you are wasting his time. Why? When you look closely at the blessings in Deuteronomy 28, God does not promise that your job will provide them. No, these blessings come from *Him.*

Realize that no human being on this earth will pay you what you are worth. So, why do you expect it from people? Why don't you expect what God said you are worth from Him? Your source is not humanity; your source is God, so receive what you are worth from heaven.

You might be thinking, *I don't know how to receive what I am due from heaven.* This is a basic conflict in the church. We don't know how to receive God's blessings; nor do we understand our worth in Christ. Remember, our heavenly Father sent His Son, Jesus, to die for us and has promised blessings to us. Yet our minds revert back to what our deceived forefathers have taught us. We choose to believe society instead of the Word of God. You are what God declared you to be, and no one can diminish you. No one can steal from you what God can't replace in abundance.

All humanity has this authority. However, we who are redeem from the curse of the Law have better promises. Not only do have the promises God gave to all humanity, but we also have t covenant of Abraham. Beyond that, we have a more exceeding precious covenant in Christ Jesus.

Think about this. Jesus employed a thief to manage His mone yet He never complained of lack. What an acid test! Take a prove thief, give him complete control of all the money you earn, ar never suffer lack in any area. Would we dare to do that? Many us probably would not, because we still look to people as our sour instead of tapping into the resources of God.

PLANT YOUR DREAM SEEDS

What can you do when achieving your dreams appear far beyond human ability? Throughout the Bible, God's people had impossible dreams. Yet I can almost hear the Lord saying to them and to you today, "I have made you and given these dream seeds to you. Now sow them, and watch what happens."

In the Bible, Elisha, the son of Shaphat, stopped plowing his field and sowed his life to become prophet Elijah's servant. Then, when God took Elijah to heaven, Elisha literally picked up Elijah's mantle and became the prophet Elisha. He had sown his dream to be like Elijah, and then went on to perform twice as many miracles as Elijah. (Read Elisha's story in 1 Kings 19–2 Kings 13.)

King David had a consuming dream in his spirit—a vision for the dwelling place of God:

> *Furthermore David the king said unto all the congregation, Solomon my son, whom alone God hath chosen, is yet young and tender, and the work is great: for the palace is not for man, but for the LORD God. Now I have prepared with all my might for the house of my God the gold for things to be made of gold, and the silver for things of silver, and the brass for things of brass, the iron for things of iron, and wood for things of wood; onyx stones, and stones to be set, glistering stones, and of divers colours, and all manner of precious stones, and marble stones in abundance. Moreover, because I have set my affection to the house of my God, I have of mine own proper good, of gold and silver, which I have given to the house of my God, over and above all that I have prepared for the holy house.*
>
> (1 Chronicles 29:1–3)

When David conquered all the enemy nations, he did not simply desire more territory. No, he wanted to exercise his might or dominion, so he could build a house for God. All his days, he was willing to be a man of bloodshed, conquering and subduing. Something inside David caused him to sow for what he dreamed. David's donation to the building of Solomon's temple was about a billion dollars in today's currency.

Today, Saudi Arabia is channeling tens of millions of dollars into building mosques around the world. Why? Because the Saudis have passion. How did they obtain the money to pursue their passion? They took hold of God's resource oil and started believing that they had the right to control it. Saudi Arabia then joined several other oil-producing nations to form a cartel called OPEC (Organization of Petroleum Exporting Countries). Together they dictate the economy of the world by raising and lowering the prices and supply of oil according to how much money they want to make. They were simply acting like human beings. Today, they still take dominion, and the rest of the world must respond to their decisions.

Americans live in a society that grants them the right of ownersh This is not true in many places across the world. Why did God g Americans such a free environment? The reason is so that we c take the world for Christ!

The decision-makers of the world are merely acting lil humans. Where did they get their authority? It is from God. A humanity has this authority. However, we who are redeemed fro the curse of the Law have better promises. Not only do we have t promises God gave to all humanity, but we also have the covena of Abraham. Beyond that, we have a more exceedingly precious covenant in Christ Jesus.

> *The earth is the LORD's, and the fulness thereof; the world, and they that dwell therein.*   (Psalm 24:1)

Now, we have not only the earth, which is the Lord's, and the fullness thereof, but we also have the delegated authority to use it according to God's purposes.

EXPECT GOD'S BEST EVEN IN NEGATIVE CIRCUMSTANCES

Let every negative situation you face produce a godly motivation for wealth. Then, extract the gold from each the crisis. For example, we will look at how the Israelites did this.

For hundreds of years, they lived under bondage. Then, when Moses heard from God, he declared that they would take Egypt's wealth when they left the country, and they did.

> *And the children of Israel did according to the word of Moses; and they borrowed of the Egyptians jewels of silver, and jewels of gold, and raiment: And the LORD gave the people favour in the sight of the Egyptians, so that they lent unto them such things as they required. And they spoiled the Egyptians.*
> (Exodus 12:35–36)

Every time God set the Israelites free from bondage and impoverishment, they received huge economic breakthroughs. That's why, in the Bible, millions of Jews could carry wealth for generations without ever working at paying jobs! Don't expect that you will experience anything less. In my life, every time I have been freed from limitation and control, I have received great economic resources. It is a biblical pattern. The Bible declares:

> *A good man leaves an inheritance for his children's children, but a sinner's wealth is stored up for the righteous. An unplowed*

field produces food for the poor, but injustice sweeps it away.
                                          (Proverbs 13:22–23 NIV)

How do we obtain sinners' wealth? Do we steal it from them? Oh, no. You don't need to steal it, because God will cause them to simply give it to you. When? You will reap this blessing when you plant the dream in your heart and tap into the giftings God has already put within you!

Do you remember when Oral Roberts announced that he would die unless God provided a certain amount of funds (millions of dollars)? Many people, especially in the United States, mocked him as a fool who blamed God for his lack of money. No, this was a contemporary person who publicly declared that God *would* make it happen. Do you remember the result? The money came to him from a dog owner, who was a gambling unbeliever! In communion with God, Oral Roberts had set his dream before the Lord, saying, "God, this *has* to work." And it did.

One of the greatest faculties you possess is the power to create. Maybe circumstances have suffocated and squashed this ability within you. It may now be frustrated and limited. Maybe you grew up in an environment that told you, "This is impossible. It will never work."

Know that your history does not define your future. The only things that matter are your dreams and the seeds you activate. Remember, you don't have to activate a fully mature oak tree. You simply need to activate an acorn (or a seed), because all oak trees in the world start as tiny acorns.

You may have heard the American pioneer stories about Johnny Appleseed, whose real name was John Chapman (1774–1845). Reportedly, for forty years, Johnny traveled the frontier planting apple trees in wild nurseries and distributing apple seeds to settlers heading west. "He wanted one thing only—to carry the apple seeds of the East to the newly cleared lands of the West that the pioneers might have the juicy fruit to eat."[3] When the settlers paid him money, he "gave [it] to the poor, bought religious books, or fed broken-down horses. More often they paid him in cast-off clothing or cornmeal."[4] Yet, he followed his dream. Then, before his death, Johnny Appleseed had the honor of seeing apple orchards span thousands of acres, which had grown from his seedlings! One could say that he lived not by how many seeds are in an apple but by how many apples are in a seed.

Don't simply judge your dream seeds by their face value. Envision their multiplied fruit! America's Declaration of Independence states,

> We hold these truths to be self-evident, that all men are created equal, that they are endowed by their Creator with certain unalienable Rights, that among these are Life, Liberty and the pursuit of Happiness.

By the term "the pursuit of happiness," the signers "meant the right to own property and to have it safeguarded. It also meant the right to strive for the good of all people, not only for one's personal happiness."[5] Americans live in a society that grants them the right of ownership. This is not true in many places across the world. Why did God give Americans such a free environment? The reason is so that we can take the world for Christ!

In life, you can ponder either how many seeds are in an apple or how many apple trees can be produced from one seed. Start thinking multiplication. Think about replenishing, subduing, and taking dominion. It's time to rule your environment. It is your right. No one on this earth can take it from you, because no earthly being gave it to you.

Compton's Interactive Encyclopedia Deluxe (The Learning Company, Inc., 1998).
Ibid.
The World Book Encyclopedia (World Book, Inc., 2000).

See the magnitude of your God! Take the limits off Him! Now, pray this as you receive the millionaire mentality of prophetic vision:

God of heaven,

I recognize that in Your Word exists limitless resources and ability. In fact, You have created me limitless in my very nature, because You made me in Your image.

Father, I believe Your Word, which says that You created me to be a fruit bearer, multiplier, replenisher, subduer, and dominator. You created and destined me to rule in this world and to take dominion. I step into that anointing right now.

This world has no voice in my dream. My dream gives voice to this world. I am Your representative, an ambassador for Christ, and the temple of the Spirit of the Lord. According to Your Word, I have the right to live in glory, honor, and dignity, which magnifies You.

Jesus, You have lifted me and released me to emulate Your life. Spirit of the Lord, reign in me. Move through me. Stir the dreams and prophetic visions within my heart, and as I plant them, I expect to reap Your promised blessings and provisions, because I choose to obey and follow You with all my heart. In Jesus' name, amen.

5

BECOME PREGNANT WITH GOD'S DREAM

It's time to get pregnant!

As you spend time fellowshipping with God, you become intimate with Him through His Holy Spirit. He then impregnates you with His dream! If you do not have a vision, or if you do but cannot activate it, then get intimate with God. Let Him fill you to overflowing with a clear direction of promise for your life! In this chapter, we will examine the third millionaire mentality principle: pregnant meditation. This key can change your life.

AS A MAN THINKS, SO IS HE

Accept the responsibility of the vision, which the Spirit of God has placed within your heart, even if you do not know what it yet. Recognize that you carry God's dream within you, and seek Him to discover it. Realize that your situation does not limit God.

Your circumstances do not dictate God's dream for your life. On the other hand, His dream will provide purpose for your life and literally free you from your challenges. Remember, God does not determine your tomorrow by your situation today.

It's important to change your thinking. You see, unless you think correctly, you will not become impregnated with the dream and the mind of God. Proverbs 23:7 tells us that *"as* [a man] *thinks in his heart, so is he"* (NKJV). What a man thinks deep down in the innermost recesses of his being dictates what he becomes. This Scripture is true of both good and bad thoughts.

The greatest hindrance to this transfer of the world's wealth to t body of Christ is their wrong beliefs. Christians think they are r worthy of great financial blessings, or they do not believe it is Go will for them to prosper. We must overcome these lies of the ener

For example, in an earlier chapter, I shared how I bega to thank and praise God on my miserable job. Soon, my wor became a joy. Countless men have left their wives and famili after becoming obsessed with other women through internet po nography and online communication via chat rooms and e-ma Thinking about being unfaithful caused them to be unfaithf So whether your thoughts are righteous or not, you become wh you think.

Likewise, many people inhibit their prophetic visions focusing on their lack of money. Not one biblical reference exi in which God stopped moving because of lack of finances. As we have discussed, He placed you on this earth to carry out His objectives. He does not give a vision to you and stop there; He also provides the means to accomplish it by pouring out wealth upon you. After all, you must have finances to accomplish His dream. This is why the Lord wants to develop the mind-set in you that you can receive His wealth! He wants to remove the limits on your financial belief system, so that you can fulfill His plans on earth.

This subject has burned within my spirit since November 1991, when the Lord instructed me to wage war on debt. He has impressed strongly upon my heart that He desires to pour out financial blessings upon His people. The greatest hindrance to this transfer of the world's wealth to the body of Christ is their wrong beliefs. Christians think they are not worthy of great financial blessings, or they do not believe it is God's will for them to prosper. We must overcome these lies of the enemy.

You see, if you change the way you *think*, you change the way you *exist*. Too many people abort the dream of the Spirit by holding on to the reality of the natural realm. Many often fear dreams, because they appear too big and impossible compared to their circumstances. However, as we read earlier, the Bible tells us that we cannot serve two masters. Either we walk in the Spirit and pursue our dreams, or we walk in the natural realm and reap the consequences of poverty.

This I say then, Walk in the Spirit, and ye shall not fulfil the lust of the flesh. For the flesh lusteth against the Spirit, and the Spirit against the flesh: and these are contrary the one to the other: so that ye cannot do the things that ye would. But if ye be led of the Spirit, ye are not under the law.

(Galatians 5:16–18)

You cannot be double-minded and expect to succeed.

> *But let him ask in faith, nothing wavering. For he that wavereth is like a wave of the sea driven with the wind and tossed. For let not that man think that he shall receive any thing of the Lord. A double minded man is unstable in all his ways.*
>
> (James 1:6–8)

Your dream must consume you. Then, God will provide the wealth to accomplish it.

THE HOLY SPIRIT BROODS OVER YOU

In the first two verses of the Bible, we read:

> *In the beginning God (prepared, formed, fashioned, and) created the heavens and the earth. The earth was without form and an empty waste, and darkness was upon the face of the very great deep. The Spirit of God was moving (hovering, brooding) over the face of the waters.*   (Genesis 1:1–2 AMP)

Since all that God is and does is perfect, God did not creat anything that is void, formless, and lacking. Therefore, I believe tha something must have happened between Genesis 1:1 and 1:2 t cause "*the earth* [to be] *without form and an empty waste.*" That's whe I believe the fall of Lucifer occurred, when Satan became God number one enemy. Otherwise, how could the earth have been voi and without form? How could darkness have been upon the face the deep, when the Bible says that there is no darkness in God?

> *This then is the message which we have heard of him, and declare unto you, that God is light, and in him is no darkness at all.*
>
> (1 John 1:5)

Therefore, this must have been when Lucifer and one-third the angels fell, which resulted in a chaotic environment.[6]

---

6. For more information on this event, please read Isaiah 14, Ezekiel 28, and Revelation 12. My book *Conquering Your Unseen Enemies: How Jesus Sets You Fr* also explains the story of the angel's fall.

Then, in Genesis 1:2, according to the original dream of God, the Holy Spirit entered the chaos and hovered over it. The word "*hover*" reminds me of what a mother hen does when she sits on her eggs and broods over them until they hatch into chicks. She envisions one form (eggs) becoming another (chicks), and she is willing to do whatever it takes to make that happen. Similarly, the Holy Spirit comes to us with God's original intention and dream for our life. Then, He says, "I am willing to incubate you until you become the person I intend for you to be and do the things I intend for you to do."

Stop thinking about your life as it now appears and think on what God has always thought, purposed, and dreamed for you. What is on God's heart concerning you? What is in His mind? What has He been thinking and dreaming about you?

The apostle Paul wrote:

[God] hath saved us, and called us with an holy calling, not according to our works, but according to his own purpose and grace, which was given us in Christ Jesus before the world began.
(2 Timothy 1:9)

The plan of God for your life was not created when you were born. His will concerning you has absolutely nothing to do with your natural birth. Before the world began, God called you for a purpose in Christ Jesus. He dreamed of you, purposed you, and had you in His Son before He created the heavens and the earth!

I believe that the most beautiful women on the face of the earth are those who are physically pregnant. They glow. Carrying life inside them does something to their spirits. The spark of incubation and growth of new life surges through the entire fabric of their beings.

Whether a man or a woman, you need to be spiritually pregnant. Carrying the energizing life of God's dream within your spirit will invigorate your entire life. It's easy to recognize people who are fulfilling their dreams. It does not matter what they face—nothing is too big for them to handle. On the other hand, to those who live only in the present—in the frustrations of today—nearly every little problem appears insurmountable.

Too many people in our society focus on the simple challenges of everyday life. That's not how God intends for us to live. He wants us to live the dream He had in mind for us even before we existed. The psalmist declared,

> *For you* [God] *created my inmost being; you knit me together in my mother's womb. I praise you because I am fearfully and wonderfully made; your works are wonderful, I know that full well. My frame was not hidden from you when I was made in the secret place, when I was woven together in the depths of the earth. Your eyes saw my unformed body; all the days ordained for me were written in your book before one of them came to be.* (Psalm 139:13–16 NIV)

Your heavenly Father has a plan for you! When you become an incubator of that dream, all things will work together for good, and your spirit will soar with hope in God. He promises His children

> *Andweknowthatallthingsworktogetherforgoodtothemthatlove God, to them who are the called according to his purpose.* (Romans 8:28)

> *Return to your fortress, you prisoners of hope; even now I announce that I will restore twice as much to you.* (Zechariah 9:12 NIV)

Even now you must renew your hope that God will restore you and breathe new life into your being.

Contrast this with a person who has a "peanut" brain. This someone who thinks small, only about what he can see. If you we to ask him, "What will you do today?" he would reply, "Oh, I'll get up, get dressed, eat breakfast, brush my teeth, and go to work."

"Then what will you do?" you might ask.

"Put in my time," he will say, "take a break, put in my time, eat lunch, put in my time, take a break, put in my time, and go back home."

"Then what?"

"Yell at the kids, eat dinner, look at the paper, watch TV, and go to bed. Then I'll wake up the next day and start over."

This mundane, limited existence is *not* the life God dreamed and purposed for us before creation! No, we need to launch out, go over the edge, and allow Him to start revealing His larger dream for us.

By the impregnation of God's dream, I do not mean what the world has to offer: a better job, houses, cars, and worldly possessions. I do not refer to making money, having it, or spending it. I am not writing about what *man* can do. This all is about discovering what is in God's mind and what He can do in your life. After all, nothing else is significant. This is at the foundation of a millionaire mentality.

BIG DREAMS IN IMPOSSIBLE CIRCUMSTANCES

Throughout the Bible, God's people carried out His dreams for their lives despite the odds. Let's examine Joseph's dream. At age seventeen, Jacob's favorite son, Joseph, dreamed of his brothers' sheaves bowing down to his. (See Genesis 37:7.) When he shared his dream with his brothers, they hated him for it. Conspiring to rid themselves of him and his dreams, they threw Joseph into a pit, then sold him into slavery. He landed in an Egyptian prison. Eventually, however, Joseph grew extremely prosperous and powerful—second only to Pharaoh. He became ruler of Egypt and lived in the palace.

> *And Pharaoh said unto his servants, Can we find such a one as this is, a man in whom the Spirit of God is? And Pharaoh said unto Joseph, Forasmuch as God hath shewed thee all this, there is none so discreet and wise as thou art: thou shalt be over my house, and according unto thy word shall all my people be ruled: only in the throne will I be greater than thou. And Pharaoh said unto Joseph, See, I have set thee over all the land of Egypt. And Pharaoh took off his ring from his hand, and put it upon Joseph's hand, and arrayed him in vestures of fine linen, and put a gold chain about his neck; and he made him to ride in the second chariot which he had; and they cried before him, Bow the knee: and he made him ruler over all the land of Egypt. And Pharaoh said unto Joseph, I am Pharaoh, and without thee shall no man lift up his hand or foot in all the land of Egypt.* (Genesis 41:38–44)

Years later in the midst of a famine, Joseph's position enabled him to provide for his father and brothers. Thus, he saved them from starvation.

What a long way Joseph came from the pit! Did you ever stop to think about how Joseph's apparently impossible circumstances were actually part of God's fulfillment of his dream? This teaches us not to become discouraged when challenges come our way. Instead, we must focus on God's plan for our lives.

Furthermore, Moses accepted God's vision for his life: delivering the Israelites from bondage. But then he tried to accomplish with his own strength by supposition. Sometimes today, we operate similarly by acting on our own assumptions.

> *And Moses was learned in all the wisdom of the Egyptians, and was mighty in words and in deeds. And when he was*

> *full forty years old, it came into his heart to visit his brethren*
> *the children of Israel. And seeing one of them suffer wrong,*
> *he defended him, and avenged him that was oppressed, and*
> *smote the Egyptian: for he supposed his brethren would have*
> *understood how that God by his hand would deliver them:*
> *but they understood not.*   (Acts 7:22–25)

Moses thought that the rest of the Israelites had heard from God, too, but they had not. You see, a dream and vision from God gives a person a private line with God.

> *And the next day he shewed himself unto them as they strove,*
> *and would have set them at one again, saying, Sirs, ye are*
> *brethren; why do ye wrong one to another? But he that did his*
> *neighbour wrong thrust him away, saying, Who made thee a*
> *ruler and a judge over us?*   (verses 26–27)

Now, Moses had the answer to this question, for he was indeed to be the ruler and judge over Israel. However, he could not express this, because they would not hear it.

---

possible circumstances and chaotic atmospheres usually round God's dreams. When fulfilling God's dreams, most ple become sidetracked with logjams of distractions.

Jesus said, "*But blessed are your eyes, for they see: and your ears, r they hear*" (Matthew 13:16). Many people see yet do not under- and. They hear but do not know the significance.

Because the Israelites did not understand Moses' vision, his dream withered. They temporarily lost the blessings his fulfilled dreams would have provided them. As a result, two entire generations of Israelites died. The first generation died when Moses acted in supposition and the people did not understand that he was their deliverer. The second generation died as they wandered in the wilderness. It took eighty years for a new generation to enter into the Promised Land.

Impossible circumstances and chaotic atmospheres usually surround God's dreams. When fulfilling God's dreams, most people become sidetracked with logjams of distractions. For example, let's say that you are praying in fellowship with God and start to perceive His vision. Then, a challenge presents itself. Instead of capturing and running with the dream you are given, you give your attention, focus, prayer life, and entire effort to this distraction. Suddenly, the question of whether your dream will manifest hinges upon overcoming this challenge.

You probably know people who are continually in conflict They go from one tragedy to the next, from worry to worry, from anxiety to anxiety, and from frustration to frustration. They do not see the broader picture, and they do not go from glory to glory as God intends.

> But we all, with open face beholding as in a glass the glory of the Lord, are changed into the same image from glory to glory, even as by the Spirit of the Lord. (2 Corinthians 3:18)

If you run with God's dream, your challenges will work themselves out. Why? Do you remember Romans 8:28, which we read earlier? *"All things work together for good to them that love God, t them who are the called according to his purpose"* (Romans 8:28 When you are following in His purpose, God orchestrates you circumstances. You do not have to tend to them yourself. N longer will your mind be occupied with challenges.

Instead, God's dream will be your all-consuming motivation. His vision will be the overriding, presiding purpose in your life. You will breathe, live, move, and have your being in it.

> *That they should seek the Lord, if haply they might feel after him, and find him, though he be not far from every one of us: for in him we live, and move, and have our being; as certain also of your own poets have said, for we are also his offspring.*
> (Acts 17:27–28)

---

ur liberation will not result from circumstances working together r you on earth. No, your liberation will come by dreaming nitlessly. Your dreams are bigger than the earth, and freedom s within them.

Your vision is bigger than your life and what you can do alone. If you do not focus your entire being on God and His dream, you will find yourself trusting in the arm of the flesh as Moses first did. Then, your own fear will become a limiting factor.

After the Holy Spirit moved upon the face of the waters (see Genesis 1:2), what happened? *"And God said, Let there be light: and there was light"* (Genesis 1:3). From chaos, God incubated His dream and spoke it forth. His Word and power holds everything together. No matter how chaotic your situation may be, rest ssured that God has a dream for you. Your challenges—whether marital disharmony, financial destruction, physical infirmity, or ocial conflicts—do not matter. Regardless of your circumstances, God's dream for you is big enough to deliver you. You must not look at or dwell upon the factors that bind you. Instead, look to the God who called you with a purpose even before your birth.

Think again about Abraham. God told Abraham that, because of his faith, He would bless all the families on the earth:

> *It was not through the law that Abraham and his offspring received the promise that he would be heir of the world, but through the righteousness that comes by faith.*
>
> (Romans 4:13 NIV)

Abraham became the heir of the world. Remember, because you now partake in the blessings of Abraham, you, too, are an heir of the world. God has destined you to rule, influence, control, and have absolute dominion. You must begin to think like it!

GOD'S DREAM FOR YOU

You might be thinking, *I'm reading* Millionaire Mentality. *I would be blessed, if I had a million dollars.* This is not a mentality of delegation but of accumulation. Don't live with a mind-set focused on what you can accumulate to satisfy your flesh. You could lose everything in an afternoon. God is not a god of accumulation. He commands us to delegate, rule, control, and take dominion. Meditate on God's purpose for you since before the foundation of the world. Enlarge the capacity and possibilities of your dream in Him.

Joseph stepped beyond the limitations of his bondage into the liberation of his dream, which God had given to him. Your liberation will not result from circumstances working together for you on earth. No, your liberation will come by dreaming limitlessly. Your dreams are bigger than the earth, and freedom lies within them. Motivation does not occur when something goes your way; it comes when you start to see (or imagine) everything get out of your way! That's when something bigger than you will start to st inside your spirit. So live beyond your circumstances. Take what God births in you—the dream seed of His revelation—and let it incubate. Brood over and meditate upon it until it forms you into who Christ wants you to be.

---

ll that God purposed for your life existed before the foundation f the earth, and He freely gives us dreams, which the Holy pirit reveals.

Remember, you must sow your dreams even in contrary environments. Don't ever wait for natural circumstances to work. If you do, this can disillusion and frustrate you. The Bible declares,

> *Hope deferred maketh the heart sick: but when the desire cometh, it is a tree of life.* (Proverbs 13:12)

When you expect and put your hope in earthly, natural results on the horizontal plane, you set yourself up for disappointment and discouragement. On the other hand, if you live in the vertical plane of God's dream, your circumstances will work together perfectly, according to His plan.

You might be asking, *How can I live this way?* Keep living in the future of your dreams. *But what about today?* Today is only the product of yesterday. Tomorrow is where you need to live. Yes, you have faith for today, but your vision is for tomorrow. This may be a whole different mind-set to you, but God's dream is greater than what you can see with your natural eyes. You must live beyond the apparent, beyond today's frustrations. You see, you can live in the present and be miserable. Alternatively, you can live in God's dream and make your present serve His future purpose. Take what you have in your hand today, and make it serve your future. The Bible commands, *"Beat your plowshares into swords and your pruninghooks into spears: let the weak say, I am strong"* (Joel 3:10).

Make your normal environment a servant that fulfills the purpose of God. Allow the dream within you to change your environment. Let your spirit rise above the ordinary and soar in God. Take the average over the edge. Never forget that you are to live, think, breathe, move, and exist in His dream arena. Be an incubator of God's dreams!

The apostle Paul wrote,

> But we speak the wisdom of God in a mystery, even the hidden wisdom, which God ordained before the world unto our glory: which none of the princes of this world knew: for had they known it, they would not have crucified the Lord of glory. But as it is written, Eye hath not seen, nor ear heard, neither have entered into the heart of man, the things which God hath prepared for them that love him. But God hath revealed them unto us by his Spirit: for the Spirit searcheth all things, yea, the deep things of God. For what man knoweth the things of a man, save the spirit of man which is in him? even so the things of God knoweth no man, but the Spirit of God. Now we have received, not the spirit of the world, but the spirit which is of God; that we might know the things that are freely given to us of God.   (1 Corinthians 2:7–12)

Paul did not preach according to his experiences. No, he spoke of God's revelation from before the foundation of the earth. He captured and communicated God's wisdom from the ages before creation. Paul said that if the demonic princes and stronghold which govern this world, had known, they would not have crucified Jesus. Neither does man—through his faculties of reason sight, and hearing—possess the capacity to know what God has prepared for those who love Him. Only the Holy Spirit knows the things of God.

> For by grace are ye saved through faith; and that not of your-selves: it is the gift of God: not of works, lest any man should boast. For we are his workmanship, created in Christ Jesus unto good works, which God hath before ordained that we should walk in them.   (Ephesians 2:8–10)

You see, those who boast say, "I have accomplished and achieved." However, those who walk in grace say, "I have received God's free gift." We are to take the dream seeds God has freely given and revealed to us, and sow them to produce fruit. Inside us, these seeds start forming, growing, and revealing what is to come. We need to become incubators and solidifiers until God's dreams manifest.

Never forget: All that God purposed for your life existed before the foundation of the earth, and He freely gives us dreams, which the Holy Spirit reveals. Nothing is more valuable than God's gifts. You cannot raise enough money to pay Him adequately for what He freely gives. It does not matter how much effort, work, and strength you exert. God says, "My purpose for your life is indepen-dent of your works. My free gift is more than you alone could ever earn in your entire lifetime."

Now, quiet your spirit as you answer these important ques-tions: What dream has God given to you? What revelation, from before the foundation of the earth, have you discovered? When you sit in God's throne room—when you fellowship and commune with Him without shame, guilt, or inferiority—what do you see? What dream does God unveil before your eyes? What has He set in eternity for you? Maybe you are thinking, *I don't have a dream; I didn't know one existed for me.* Oh, but it does indeed exist for you!

God has always had your dream in His mind. It's time for *you* to get it into *yours*!

RECORD THE VISION AND KEEP IT BEFORE YOUR EYES

When a vision comes, expect your life to change. Habakkuk declared:

> *I will stand my watch and set myself on the rampart, and watch to see what He will say to me, and what I will answer when I am corrected. Then the* LORD *answered me and said: "Write the vision and make it plain on tablets, that he may run who reads it. For the vision is yet for an appointed time; but at the end it will speak, and it will not lie. Though it tarries, wait for it; because it will surely come, it will not tarry."*
> (Habakkuk 2:1–3 NKJV)

When God's vision comes to you, it will correct your thinking. Be sure to record the vision and keep it before your eyes, and, if necessary, the eyes of others. Never forget its significance in your life. Don't let the things of this world—such as advertising campaigns, sales gimmicks, and humanistic promotions—distract you or cause you to lose focus. Jesus warned,

> *And the cares of this world, and the deceitfulness of riches, and the lusts of other things entering in, choke the word, and it becometh unfruitful. And these are they which are sown on good ground; such as hear the word, and receive it, and bring forth fruit, some thirtyfold, some sixty, and some an hundred.*
> (Mark 4:19–20)

If you don't keep your focus on your vision, your enemy wil entice you through both things and people, saying, "Follow me. In this way, he will tempt you to veer off course. If you submi then you will not know the joy of fulfillment. You see, God di not design you to find fulfillment in worldly things. This never has been—and never will be—God's plan for you.

When you find God's dream for your life, let it correct and reprove you. Allow it to bring you to honesty. Allow it to deal with the areas of your life that you count significant and valuable. Let it break your outer man and your inner man.

When a man truly has a dream, in the end, the dream has the man. It becomes his only focus—as if nothing else exists. Many people are still in the first stage of dream living, saying, "I will have a dream. I will hear it." This is not good enough. You must know the dream, seize it, and allow it to change your thinking. Let it rearrange your entire being, so you can focus on God's eternal picture. Once His dream impregnates you, you no longer have it—it has you. If you let the vision have you, then you are no longer yourself. Now, you and the dream are one. No one can disconnect a person from his God-given dream.

Although Joseph's brothers tried, they could not separate him from his dream. You see, they were not trying to get rid of Joseph; they were trying to get rid of his dream. And, since his dream was within him, they physically threw Joseph into the pit.

And his brethren said to him, Shalt thou indeed reign over us? or shalt thou indeed have dominion over us? And they hated him yet the more for his dreams, and for his words.... And when they saw him afar off, even before he came near unto them, they conspired against him to slay him. And they said one to another, Behold, this dreamer cometh. Come now therefore, and let us slay him, and cast him into some pit, and we will say, Some evil beast hath devoured him: and we shall see what will become of his dreams.

(Genesis 37:8, 18–20)

PRAY IN THE SPIRIT TO RECEIVE GOD'S ANSWER

Another way to receive the revelation of God's dream for your life is by fellowshipping with God in the Spirit. Jesus said, "*God is a Spirit: and they that worship him must worship him in spirit and in truth*" (John 4:24). How do you get God's vision? How does it come into your spirit? By praying in the Holy Spirit. I love the language of the Spirit of God. Although I cannot understand it, it changes my entire being.

> *For he that speaketh in an unknown tongue speaketh not unto men, but unto God: for no man understandeth him; howbeit in the spirit he speaketh mysteries* [God's divine secrets].
> (1 Corinthians 14:2)

When I pray in my native tongue, it is from the arena of my own understanding. However, when I pray in the Spirit of God, I am praying in the arena of the unknown. It is beyond the threshold of anything I could ever imagine. Our prayers in the Spirit are not possibilities prayers but absolute realities. How can this be? It is because I am praying according to the mind and purpose of God. As I pray in the Spirit, God reveals my dreams to me in the form of a picture or perception.

> *Wherefore let him that speaketh in an unknown tongue pray that he may interpret. For if I pray in an unknown tongue, my spirit prayeth, but my understanding is unfruitful. What is it then? I will pray with the spirit, and I will pray with the understanding also: I will sing with the spirit, and I will sing with the understanding also.* (1 Corinthians 14:13–15)

God has designed us to speak in the language of His Spirit and to become pregnant with His dreams. The millionaire mentality has nothing to do with getting more money in your wallet or bank account. It has to do with your mind-set, having the capacity to hear and receive the mind of Christ. Listen to Him and allow Him to teach you. Earlier, we read part of the following passage in the Bible:

> Come ye near unto me, hear ye this; I have not spoken in secret from the beginning; from the time that it was, there am I: and now the LORD God, and his Spirit, hath sent me. Thus saith the LORD, thy Redeemer, the Holy One of Israel; I am the LORD thy God which teacheth thee to profit, which leadeth thee by the way that thou shouldest go.   (Isaiah 48:16–17)

These verses reveal that prosperity, increase, and success in life come from a combination of teaching and learning. It is not an event. For example, when it comes to careers, we know that in order to qualify for a certain job, we must learn specific fundamentals about the business and/or technologies. As we receive teaching from others with experience in these fields, we can then practice our new knowledge and skills. Eventually, we become proficient in these skills. Thus, as we accept teaching, we progress into deeper levels of experience.

_____

you are experiencing frustration and a never-ending drone of misery in your daily routine, it is time to modify it! Without radical change, you will continue operating in the same way, and you will reap similar harvests over and over.

This is God's desire for us in every area of life. He wants to teach us how to experience deeper levels of His blessings. God will teach you to profit and lead you in fulfilling His plan for your life. First, however, you must be willing to accept His teaching and then follow it. When you do, God will release wealth that will hurry to fulfill your prophetic purpose. Stay alert in prayer to recognize the leading of the Holy Spirit. Then follow His voice.

THE FINAL PROOF

No matter what you do, be certain that you do not allow your dream-driven life to violate the proven principles of God's Word. Let God's Word be the guide in all you do. For example, follow God's Word regarding worry. You cannot receive the wisdom of God while the worries of everyday life occupy your mind. Instead, you must let the peace of God rule.

> *Be careful for nothing; but in every thing by prayer and supplication with thanksgiving let your requests be made known unto God. And the peace of God, which passeth all understanding, shall keep your hearts and minds through Christ Jesus.* (Philippians 4:6–7)

You must never allow an anxious thought to remain in you mind. Jesus said:

> *Therefore I tell you, do not worry about your life, what you will eat or drink; or about your body, what you will wear. Is not life more than food, and the body more than clothes? Look at the birds of the air; they do not sow or reap or store away in barns, and yet your heavenly Father feeds them. Are you not much more valuable than they?* (Matthew 6:25–26 NIV)

Anchor your faith in the Bible's simple and practical trut
Keep the Word of God in your heart at all times.

> *This book of the law shall not depart out of thy mouth; but thou shalt meditate therein day and night, that thou mayest observe to*

do according to all that is written therein: for then thou shalt make thy way prosperous, and then thou shalt have good success.

(Joshua 1:8)

SUCCESS IS FOUND IN YOUR DAILY ROUTINE

Many say their dreams are pie in the sky, believing that they will never happen. Have you ever heard anyone say that he will follow his dreams when his ship comes home, meaning when he gets rich? This type of thinking is very dangerous. Every day around you, harvests are yours to reap. Daily, therefore, you should be moving in or toward your field to reap it. You see, your daily routine and thoughts will cause you either to fail or to succeed. The mentality of leaving your life to fate or whatever comes will set you up for failure. This is a sure way to avoid fulfilling your dream. You must have a take-charge attitude and lifestyle.

Daily, you must establish a routine of harnessing your mind to correct judgments and actions. The following Scripture has been a great measuring rod in my life:

Whoso keepeth the commandment shall feel no evil thing: and a wise man's heart discerneth both time and judgment. Because to every purpose there is time and judgment, therefore the misery of man is great upon him. (Ecclesiastes 8:5–6)

If you are experiencing frustration and a never-ending drone of misery in your daily routine, it is time to modify it! Without radical change, you will continue operating in the same way, and you will reap similar harvests over and over.

Now is the time to renew your mind. Remember, God is carrying out His purpose according to His timing and decisions. Daily get your mind in gear. All of creation is waiting for you to renew your mind so that you can take charge of it.

> *For the creation waits in eager expectation for the children of*
> *God to be revealed.*   (Romans 8:19 NIV)

Romans 12:2 says, "*Be not conformed to this world: but be ye transformed by the renewing of your mind, that ye may prove what is that good, and acceptable, and perfect, will of God.*" You can experience a personal renovation of your mind. As you keep the Word of God foremost in your thoughts and speech, you change. It is like stripping old paint from a wooden antique chair: You remove layer by layer until the original wood fully emerges. Then, in its restored condition, the antique's true value is clear. To prove and see the Word of God fully manifest in your life, you must renew your mind! You will experience God's awesome Word in action when you daily pursue a renewed mind. Truth will withstand every test!

Once you are fully living His dream, you might need to change your millionaire mentality into a billionaire mentality! Please pray this as we close our discussion on pregnant meditation:

Father God,

   Your Word clarifies that my thinking is critical. Please help me to renew my mind, to conform it not to the world but to the truth in Your Word. Help me to rely on You and not to worry or become distracted with the cares of this world.

   Lord, restore me and breathe new life into me. Impregnate me with Your vision for my life as I become more intimate with You. Help me to obey Your Word by praying both in the Holy Spirit and with my own understanding. Let my prayers be fruitful to accomplish that which You desire.

   Strengthen me so that I am not double-minded. Help me to focus all that I have and all that I am on You and Your prophetic vision. Father, let me live, move, and have my being in You. Cause me to become an incubator of Your dream seeds. When challenges come, may I not become discouraged. Help me to remember that when I follow Your purpose, You will orchestrate my circumstances. Energize me with renewed hope, that Your dreams for me *will* come to pass. In Jesus' name, amen.

6

PROCLAIM GOD'S WORDS TO RELEASE WEALTH

We began our study of the millionaire mentality principles with the *purpose* of wealth. What is the purpose of wealth? It is to establish God's covenant. Then we progressed into the principles of *prophetic vision* and *pregnant meditation*. What is your prophetic vision? This is God's plan for your life, which He conceived before the foundation of the world. How do you discover how to achieve His objectives? You allow the Holy Spirit to impregnate you with power and wisdom, and you meditate on His truth.

The next millionaire mentality principle is *proclamation*. This is declaring that your vision will manifest and provisions will flow into your life. Few people recognize the power of this biblical principle.

THE CREATIVE POWER OF PROCLAMATION

To release your provision, you must proclaim your dream or vision. What can you accomplish through a proclamation? To answer this question, let's examine the results of God's own Words, or His proclamations. The first chapter of Genesis describes how God spoke the world into existence. Simply by the power of His Words, God created light; the sky, or heavens; the earth; the seas; vegetation; the sun, moon, and stars; and the animals. How could His Word have such power? It is because God and His Word are One.

> *In the beginning was the Word, and the Word was with God, and the Word was God. The same was in the beginning with God. All things were made by him; and without him was not any thing made that was made. In him was life; and the life was the light of men. And the light shineth in darkness; and the darkness comprehended it not....And the Word was made flesh, and dwelt among us, (and we beheld his glory, the glory as of the only begotten of the Father,) full of grace and truth.*
>
> (John 1:1–5, 14)

While we may not fully comprehend it, this passage explain that Jesus is the Word and that the Word is God. The words c God and Jesus, then, contain all their power and glory.

Furthermore, the Bible states that God's spoken Word is sti effective:

> *God, who at sundry times and in divers manners spake in time past unto the fathers by the prophets, hath in these last days spoken unto us by his Son, whom he hath appointed heir of all things, by whom also he made the worlds; who being the brightness of his glory, and the express image of his person, and upholding all things by the word of his power, when he*

*had by himself purged our sins, sat down on the right hand of
the Majesty on high.*   (Hebrews 1:1–3)

God's spoken Word ("rhema" in Hebrew) "upholds" all things;
it is the binding force by which God holds everything together.
This simple truth means that God's Word literally holds you
together! Words are a tool God uses to create. He holds everything together by His Word. The natural man does not understand this. God said,

*For my thoughts are not your thoughts, neither are your ways
my ways, saith the LORD. For as the heavens are higher than
the earth, so are my ways higher than your ways, and my
thoughts than your thoughts.*   (Isaiah 55:8–9)

Since God made us in His image, our words have His creative
power. This is the power of proclamation. When we proclaim in
alignment with God's purpose—not according to our circumstances—our mind will begin to conform to His thoughts. You
see, when the Word of God comes, it corrects. The truth of the
Word exposes our errors. It allows us to recognize wrong perspectives and ungodly attitudes. With truth comes reproof.

*All Scripture is God-breathed and is useful for teaching, rebuk-
ing, correcting and training in righteousness, so that the servant
of God may be thoroughly equipped for every good work.*
                              (2 Timothy 3:16–17 NIV)

God's Word equips us to carry out His vision for our lives.

ARE YOU DECLARING YOUR BELIEF?

Do you declare what you believe? If so, what happens when
you do so? Does God affirm the words you speak? If not, what you
believe and proclaim may be wrong. There are many very sincere
people who are sincerely deceived. Sincerity is not an earmark of

truth. Remember, even the demons sincerely believe that Jesus is Lord. *"Thou believest that there is one God; thou doest well: the devils also believe, and tremble"* (James 2:19).

When we proclaim in alignment with God's purpose—not accordir to our circumstances—our mind will begin to conform to H thoughts. You see, when the Word of God comes, it corrects. T truth of the Word exposes our errors.

Traveling around the world, I have met many kinds of people I have found that some of the most sincere people are Muslim They are earnest, committed, loyal, and faithful. However, wher I have asked them to pray to Muhammad for healing, they pra but are not healed; their diseases persist in spite of their words They also have no permanent assurance of salvation based upo the confession of their faith. The reason is because they do nc believe God's *true* Word. Therefore, their sincerity does not induc God to bring them to salvation. What does move God? A heart c faith in the truth. What does faith consist of? Faith is a combina tion of heart belief, mouth declaration, and corresponding actior of obedience to God.

> *That if thou shalt confess with thy mouth the Lord Jesus, and shalt believe in thine heart that God hath raised him from the dead, thou shalt be saved. For with the heart man believeth*

unto righteousness; and with the mouth confession is made unto salvation. (Romans 10:9–10)

For as the body without the spirit is dead, so faith without works is dead also. (James 2:26)

This is for everyone. We must declare our faith and speak the truth. Are you obeying God and passing His tests regarding your words, or are your words negative and full of defeat? Do you say, "Oh, God, I cannot take any more," to which He responds, "Then, I cannot give any more to you"?

Do not adopt the mind-set that the pressures are too great and your challenges are more than you can handle. This is not true. God promises:

There hath no temptation taken you but such as is common to man: but God is faithful, who will not suffer you to be tempted above that ye are able; but will with the temptation also make a way to escape, that ye may be able to bear it. (1 Corinthians 10:13)

Do not measure the size of the conflict you face by your strength alone; measure the size of the conflict you face in comparison to the immensity of God's strength. The apostle Paul declared about Jesus:

But [Jesus] said to me, "My grace is sufficient for you, for my power is made perfect in weakness." Therefore I will boast all the more gladly about my weaknesses, so that Christ's power may rest on me. (2 Corinthians 12:9 NIV)

The day you declare, "I cannot deal with this," is the day you become trapped. When this happens, no one can free you. Your only way of escape then is to bow your knees to God and to seek His divine intervention.

Facing conflict can cause frustration, disappointment, disillusionment, and discouragement. Because you feel that you cannot handle any more, you simply want to quit. The pressures are too great, the day is too long, and the distress is insurmountable. However, the fact is, God uses pressures to see if you will live by His Word. The Scriptures say that if you cannot run with footmen, how then will you run with horsemen? If you feel defeated, as if you are standing in ankle-deep water, how will you ever hope to swim?

> *If thou hast run with the footmen, and they have wearied thee, then how canst thou contend with horses? and if in the land of peace, wherein thou trustedst, they wearied thee, then how wilt thou do in the swelling of Jordan?*   (Jeremiah 12:5)

PROCLAIM FINANCES FOR THE VISION

Think about Job's challenges in the Bible. During all his suffering, he had many opportunities to curse God and die. However, he refused to do so. Job retained his integrity before God. He passed the test when he vowed and proclaimed God's Word, saying:

> *Thou shalt make thy prayer unto him, and he shall hear thee, and thou shalt pay thy vows. Thou shalt also decree a thing, and it shall be established unto thee: and the light shall shine upon thy ways. When men are cast down, then thou shalt say, There is lifting up; and he shall save the humble person.*
> (Job 22:27–29)

As a result, awesome breakthroughs took place in Job's life. His family and wealth increased more than ever before. At the end of his life, he had twice as much as he had. *"After Job had prayed for his friends, the LORD restored his fortunes and gave him twice as much as he had before"* (Job 42:10 NIV). Once you discover the power declaration, you can declare realities not only for yourself but for people around you.

The challenge we often face concerning financial declarations is that we do not fully believe in the power of our spoken words. We fail to believe what God's Word says about the creative ability of words. Because many factors affect our environment, we do not have the confidence, in the midst of chaos, to declare God's will. We do not believe that we will see His purposes accomplished as He speaks.

DECLARE THE VISION AND THE PROVISION

Each year, in October, November, and December, I start praying that God would reveal His vision for the next calendar year. I ask to know the purpose in which I am to walk, and the plan to implement it. Also, before the first of every year, I vow in my heart to meet my "giving goal" during the next year. Then I proclaim the purpose and vision God has revealed to me. Also, I decree the finances to be released, so that I may accomplish God's objectives that year. For twenty years I have done this.

Whenever I give to the Lord, I write on the offering envelopes my vision and giving goal vow for that year. I remind Him, "God, this is my vow. I am fulfilling Your purpose in this earth. Now, fulfill the words that I have declared in the financial arena." It's interesting to see what happens throughout that year. Sometimes the amount of money God releases to me for giving is amazing! For example, in 1996, I underestimated how God would move financially, and God exceeded my vow by 250 percent! You might be wondering if I had any natural ways of making this happen. Absolutely not. How could this be? It is because the power of proclamation works.

It is possible to cross financial thresholds when you tie money God's purpose and prove to Him that He can trust you. God is eager to release finances if He knows that, when you receive them, you will give His part back to Him. The blessing of provision results when you...

+ Align yourself with God's vision and purpose.
+ Proclaim your vision and provision into being.
+ Declare your vow and give to God.

Then, you will see the purpose and will of God accomplished in your life. Are you ready to step into supernatural breakthroughs? Remember...

> *Thou shalt remember the* LORD *thy God: for it is he that giveth thee power to get wealth, that he may establish his covenant which he sware unto thy fathers, as it is this day.*
>
> (Deuteronomy 8:18)

Provision follows vision; it does not follow need. We will further discuss this topic in the next chapter. However, let me say this: Most people put their needs on their prayer lists. Instead, why not put their vision?

As you pray, forecast the future. Take your vision before God, proclaim your provision, and declare your vow. Remember, your words bring life or death to your vision. *"Death and life are in the power of the tongue: and they that love it shall eat the fruit thereof"* (Proverbs 18:21).

I am confident that the church has not experienced a crashing wave of increase because it has not remained in faithful alignment with God's vision.

THE VOICE OF MONEY

Do you realize that money has a voice? Have you ever spoken to yourself about your financial situation? Most people mutter about money. Why? You must realize that money speaks! Without recognizing it, you can find yourself repeating what you've heard; and soon, those thoughts may come into existence. Remember, your words carry creative power. By proclaiming the negative thoughts of money, you can severely cripple your finances. Let me explain.

---

member, your words carry creative power. By proclaiming the gative thoughts of money, you can severely cripple your finances.

One day, I was standing in line behind a man at a checkout counter when I noticed he was having difficulty paying for his merchandise. Peering into his wallet, he appeared to be arguing with himself about what he was seeing. I moved a little closer to watch and listen.

Every credit card he looked at created a different grumbling within the man. His attitude ranged from anger to fear, from frustration to hopelessness. Surprisingly, he forecasted the financial failure of his future children. As he continued leafing through his billfold, he came to his pay stub. Then he blurted out that he hated his job. He wished the _____ job would _____. He removed his cash and, after mumbling another self-destructive prophecy, paid the cashier.

Before leaving the store, he said to the clerk, "With all this, how can I ever afford to get married? My girlfriend just wants to settle down, get married, and start a family. I don't know how anybody can afford to be married, let alone have kids!"

Looking at the cashier's wedding ring, he asked, "Do you have any kids?"

She replied, "Why do you think I'm behind this register? You don't think I want to be here, do you? My husband and I just pass each other in the night between jobs."

"See, I'll be darned if I'm going to live like this!" he replied. "My kids will never know me. Well, I guess not until they want some of my money, too!"

Clenching the wallet in his hand, he waved it at her as he walked off.

Then, it was my turn in line. As I approached the register, I said, "Wow, what was his problem?"

She replied, "What do people expect from me? I work here only to try to make ends meet. It is no wonder that people end up being shot on their jobs. Just look at that guy! He is flipped out and I have my own money problems!"

As I walked away from the counter, I looked into my own bill fold, wondering, *Am I this frustrated, too?*

That night I taught at a financial freedom conference. My topic was on tapping the money gap, which I have since developed into a tape series. I explained that between the cost of making a product and its sale price is a gap called profit. The thrust of my message that night was exploring why we spend so much of our money giving profit to others when God promised to teach *us* to profit.

> *Thus saith the* Lord, *thy Redeemer, the Holy One of Israel;*
> *I am the* Lord *thy God which teacheth thee to profit, which*
> *leadeth thee by the way that thou shouldest go.*
>
> (Isaiah 48:17)

At the meeting, I thought, *Let's see what happens to this assembly of Christians when I ask them to take out their cash/checkbook credit cards, and to look at them.* As I instructed them to do so, some people looked angry. Fear came over others. Some were astonished, and others were probably thinking, *Here we go. He is going to take an offering!* Immediately the atmosphere became heavy. To lighten matters, I joked, "Fear not! I'm not taking an offering!" Some giggled, others sighed with relief, but some were still skeptical. The atmosphere became a little lighter but not very much.

I thought, *If this is how the church responds before even looking in their wallets, what will happen when they open them?* I asked them to stand with all the finances they had with them—cash, credit cards, etc.—in hand. It took time for some of them to comply. Others were obstinate, refusing to do it! Over and over, I assured them I was not taking an offering and not to fear. Finally, they all were standing with money in hand.

Then I asked them to look at me and not at what was in their hands. Now the stage was set. My test was finally about to begin. I said, "Close your eyes and release yourself from any confusion or fear, in Jesus' name! Now open your eyes, and look at your credit card(s), then your money, and then your checkbook. Okay, stop, and look at me!"

As each looked at me, I simply asked, "How many of you had fearful, frustrated, or anxious thoughts? Did looking at your money spark any angry or accusing thoughts? You may even have had thoughts that forecasted a negative future. If you experienced any negative thought just now, raise your hand."

About 80 percent of the people lifted their hands. Then, the other 20 percent raised their hands after I explained to them how to recognize a negative thought. Therefore, 100 percent of the people in church had received a negative thought!

You might be wondering what this all is about. Are you ready? Can you stand another new thought? Well, ready or not, here it comes!

After they all acknowledged that they had negative thoughts, I told them to turn in their Bibles to Ecclesiastes 10:19:

> *A feast is made for laughter, and wine maketh merry: but money answereth all things.*　　　(Ecclesiastes 10:19)

Then I said to the people, "Now repeat after me, 'Money answers!' Say it again, 'Money answers!' Now, what does it answer?"

Many replied, "All things," but it didn't appear that they knew what this meant. So I continued, explaining what had happened when they looked at their money. In their thoughts, they had heard money speak to them, or answer them, in response to each person's previous thoughts or words spoken about his or her money. Money did not ask any questions, nor did it initiate any conversations. No, the Word of God says that money answers.

I know this might be new to you, but when was the last time money answered you? Please continue reading, because this can forever change how you allow your money to answer you.

Then I asked the people, "Do you like how your money talks to you? Do you allow everything to speak to you that way, and do nothing about it?"

I could see the revelation dawn on some of them. They realized that they had negative thoughts when they looked at their money.

I also saw the doubt on some faces who still probably questioned me, so I asked them to turn to Genesis 2:16–17. We read the following:

> *And the LORD God commanded the man, saying, Of every tree of the garden thou mayest freely eat: but of the tree of the knowledge of good and evil, thou shalt not eat of it: for in the day that thou eatest thereof thou shalt surely die.*

Then I asked, "Did the forbidden tree produce apples, pears, or oranges?" Obviously it did not produce any of these. I explained that it produced *knowledge*, which mankind could ingest! We know that the fall of man occurred in the garden of Eden when Adam and Eve ingested this knowledge. Suddenly they understood good and evil. But God wanted them to avoid this knowledge. Why? One of the reasons was that He did not want mankind to experience negative thoughts.

You see, after Adam and Eve disobeyed God by eating of the forbidden tree, they began to experience the first negative thoughts:

> *Then the eyes of both of them were opened, and they realized they were naked; so they sewed fig leaves together and made coverings for themselves. Then the man and his wife heard the sound of the* Lord *God as he was walking in the garden in the cool of the day, and they hid from the* Lord *God among the trees of the garden. But the* Lord *God called to the man, "Where are you?" He answered, "I heard you in the garden, and I was afraid because I was naked; so I hid."*
>
> (Genesis 3:7–10 NIV)

Suddenly, Adam's and Eve's physical nakedness produced fear. What they saw and heard in their natural environment caused negative thoughts. Similarly, physical money can arouse negative thoughts in you, as it did in all the people at my financial meeting that night.

Because of the fall of man, it is common for us to receive thoughts from the enemy through our physical environment. Today, when some people cross a bridge, they entertain the thought of jumping over the edge. Others see a river and feel as if they are drowning. Still others step onto an elevator and sense that they will fall; or they board a plane and think it will crash. These are fears, or phobias, that the devil speaks to people through the physical realm. Money answers us in a similar way but not with an audible voice.

After explaining this at my meeting, I said, "Now, we must ask ourselves, 'Can I change money's answer?'" Now I had their attention.

Immediately, I reminded them of Jesus' words in Mark 11:23:

For verily I say unto you, That whosoever shall say unto this mountain, Be thou removed, and be thou cast into the sea; and shall not doubt in his heart, but shall believe that those things which he saith shall come to pass; he shall have whatsoever he saith.

I said, "Stand up. Now, speak to your money. Tell it how you want it to answer you from now on! In Jesus' name! Do you get it? Yes, you speak, then your money will say, 'Yes, sir' or 'Yes, ma'am!' Now, take out your money again, and get ready to tell it what kind of answers you want it to speak from now on!"

Then, I led them in the following prayer:

In Jesus' name, money, you will never speak back to me like that again. I am your master, and you are my servant. I tell you where to go, and you go. I tell you when to come, and you come. From now on, you will answer all things with, "Yes! I bless my master with abundance!" Now, money, if I ever hear you answer me again with disrespect and negativity, I will discard you and get some more! Then you will never have the privilege of serving me again!

Silence filled the room. I could have heard a pin drop.

"Look at your money once more," I said. "Tell me if it speaks negatively to you again."

There was a short silence. Then the meeting erupted with shouts of joy, clapping, and thanksgiving to God. The people had once again understood God's Word, acted on it, and saw the results.

Now it is your turn. Take out your money, credit cards, and checkbook. Look at them. Then listen. Yes, you know what to do next. Pray this prayer with me:

Father,

I believe I am not simply existing on the earth. You have called me with a divine purpose and ordained me to inherit Your every promise. Now, I speak Your purpose and vision into being. I proclaim Your plan into existence. I know You will teach me to profit, and You will lead me in the way I should go.

My presence is proof that You bless Your people. You have blessed me coming in and going out. I am the head and not the tail. Whatever I put my hand to prospers. I shout aloud, "The Lord takes pleasure in the prosperity of His servants! The Lord takes pleasure in the prosperity of *me*, His servant."

I declare to You, Father, the vision that is in my heart, and I speak forth that it *will* come to pass. I release wealth, for it is Yours and will serve Your vision. When I receive it, Lord, I will sow into Your kingdom's work again.

Now, I speak to my money. In Jesus' name, I command it to answer me with respect and without any back talk. I am a child of the Most High God. Money must serve me and the prophetic vision my God has called me to fulfill. From now on, I will not entertain any negative thoughts of the enemy through my money.

Thank You, God, for giving authority to me to proclaim Your will in the earth today. In Jesus' name, amen.

7

RELEASE VISION-DRIVEN PROVISION

Many people do not understand the next millionaire-mental-principle—provision. For years, I labored under wrong thinking in this area, and my visions suffered from it. But I believe this simple revelation will revolutionize your finances, as it did mine.

THERE IS NO PROVISION WITHOUT VISION

First, let's consider the term *provision*. The prefix *pro* means "for or on behalf of." Provision, then, must be released on behalf of a vision to fulfill it. Now, if you do not have a vision, why have provision? You don't need it unless you have a vision!

You see, there are three motivations for wealth: need, greed, and vision.

Some people have such great need that they strive for wealth, believing it will satisfy their emptiness. Others simply desire to be rich, because they are greedy. A lustful motivation to gain wealth drives both types of people. When they obtain their goal, sorrow comes with it. Their pain is directly related to their love of money.

Your heavenly Father is not against your having wealth. However, He does not want wealth or the pursuit of it to control your life! Clearly, His Word warns against the love of money and the all-consuming motivation to acquire wealth.

> *But godliness with contentment is great gain. For we brought nothing into the world, and we can take nothing out of it. But if we have food and clothing, we will be content with that. People who want to get rich fall into temptation and a trap and into many foolish and harmful desires that plunge people into ruin and destruction. For the love of money is a root of all kinds of evil. Some people, eager for money, have wandered from the faith and pierced themselves with many griefs ["sorrows" (KJV)].*   (1 Timothy 6:6–10 NIV)

The great wealth that God desires to pour into your life to fulfill his vision far surpasses meeting your current needs. In fact, frantically working simply to meet your needs is not even close to His best for you. He does not bless this kind of cursed motivation.

On the other hand, some people receive visions from God. Instead of need or greed as their driving force, they desire to see God's vision fulfilled. They want to see what God can build. As these people move toward their visions, God blesses the work their hands. With the blessing comes no sorrow, according to Proverbs 10:22, which we studied earlier.

The great wealth that God desires to pour into your life to fulfill His vision far surpasses meeting your current needs. In fact, frantically working simply to meet your needs is not even close to His best for you. He does not bless this kind of cursed motivation. Instead, God intends for wealth to follow you—not for you to follow wealth.

Jesus said signs follow believers:

> And these signs shall follow them that believe; in my name shall they cast out devils; they shall speak with new tongues; they shall take up serpents; and if they drink any deadly thing, it shall not hurt them; they shall lay hands on the sick, and they shall recover.…And they went forth, and preached every where, the Lord working with them, and confirming the word with signs following. Amen.   (Mark 16:17–18, 20)

Similarly, wealth will follow you when you obey God. It is a by-product of following your God-given vision. This is what I call vision-driven provision. Remember, God is your source. When you seek Him first, He adds everything else to you:

> But seek ye first the kingdom of God, and his righteousness; and all these things shall be added unto you.
>
> (Matthew 6:33)

This basic principle appears all throughout the Bible.

BIBLICAL EXAMPLES OF VISION-DRIVEN PROVISION

The old covenant Scriptures contain many examples of supernatural provision from God. Let's examine some of these now, starting with recalling some of our study on the Israelites, then moving on to the lives of Abraham, Isaac, and Jacob.

THE ISRAELITES NEEDED TO PASS GOD'S TESTS

Daily, God provided manna for the Israelites. Remember, they had to wander in the wilderness for forty years to learn that man does not live by bread alone but by every word from God. The Israelites needed to realize that they were not to live by, or focus on, material things. Instead, God's words and His visions were to be their focus. Only when they focused on Him would provision come. Israel had to see God differently. They needed to open their eyes to see that God Himself was their provision.

GOD BLESSED ALL NATIONS THROUGH ABRAHAM

Think again about Abraham. When his name was still Abram, he was given a vision and a purpose.

> Now the Lord had said to Abram: "Get out of your country, from your family and from your father's house, to a land that I will show you. I will make you a great nation; I will bless you and make your name great; and you shall be a blessing. I will bless those who bless you, and I will curse him who curses you; and in you all the families of the earth shall be blessed."
>
> (Genesis 12:1–3 NKJV)

God's purpose was to create a great nation from Abram that would bless all humanity.

In those days, no knowledge of God or Jehovah existed. In fact, Abram's father, Terah, worshipped pagan idols:

> And Joshua said unto all the people, Thus saith the Lord God of Israel, Your fathers dwelt on the other side of the flood in old time, even Terah, the father of Abraham, and the father of Nachor: and they served other gods. And I took your father Abraham from the other side of the flood, and led him throughout all the land of Canaan.
>
> (Joshua 24:2–3)

No one had told Abram about God, so God gave Abram a personal encounter with Himself. He made a new covenant with Abram and supplied him with supernatural provision. Father God promised Abram:

> Lift up now thine eyes, and look from the place where thou art northward, and southward, and eastward, and westward: for all the land which thou seest, to thee will I give it, and to thy seed for ever. And I will make thy seed as the dust of the earth: so that if a man can number the dust of the earth, then shall thy seed also be numbered. Arise, walk through the land in the length of it and in the breadth of it; for I will give it unto thee.   (Genesis 13:14–17)

Just think: God promised to give to Abram gifts, which he had not worked for, strove for, or qualified for. Abram's only requirement was to believe that God would fulfill His promise. However, Abram had a difficult time trusting God. Already in old age, he and his wife were childless.

Then, when Abram was ninety-nine years old, and his wife, Sarai, was ninety, God changed Abram's name to Abraham, which means "father of many nations" (see Genesis 17:5), and Sarai's name to Sarah, which means "princess of many nations" (see Genesis 17:15). Now, realize that God renamed them one year before their son, Isaac, was born. (See Genesis 17:21.) What a prophetic vision this was!

How do you react to promises like these? Do you see God's vision or do you see what limits you from receiving His promises? Do you respond, "Well, God, I hear what You are saying, but what about _____?"

At first, Abraham challenged God about this vision. Through supernatural intervention, God had blessed him with cattle, silver, and gold that he hadn't worked for. (See Genesis 13:2.) Yet, he complained in Genesis 15:2–3, "God, You have given these financial blessings to me—and that's wonderful—but where is my child? How can I be the father of many nations when I have no son or blood heirs?"

How did God respond to Abraham? He simply reiterated His vision and promised to fulfill it:

> *"Look now toward heaven, and count the stars if you are able to number them." And He said to him, "So shall your descendants be." And [Abraham] believed in the LORD, and He accounted it to him for righteousness.*
>
> (Genesis 15:5–6 NKJV)

Finally, Abraham believed in the vision. His heart had to connect to God to release heaven's provision. If, instead, he had remained in the natural realm of life, Abraham would not have accomplished God's vision to become whom God had called him

---

We have seen that no matter how long the delay, God will interve and fulfill His promises. He promised to bless Jacob with blessings of Abraham, and no one could stop Him. Although blessings were delayed, they were not denied.

to be. He would not have had the faith, voice, and influence th we still recognize today. Without his spiritual encounters wi God, Abraham would not have fulfilled God's purpose. God h a vision for Abraham's life, and in every step He supplied t provision. Remember, Jesus Christ came through the lineage

Abraham. Think about it, God actually provided for *all* humanity *through* Abraham!

ISAAC DISCOVERED THAT ABUNDANCE FOLLOWS GOD'S PROMISES

When Abraham died, he left nothing to his son Isaac. Abraham had experienced famine, and, in Genesis 26:1, the Bible declares that Isaac also lived in a land of terrible famine. Yet God promised to bless Isaac, saying:

> *Sojourn in this land, and I will be with thee, and will bless thee; for unto thee, and unto thy seed, I will give all these countries, and I will perform the oath which I sware unto Abraham thy father; and I will make thy seed to multiply as the stars of heaven, and will give unto thy seed all these countries; and in thy seed shall all the nations of the earth be blessed.*
>
> (Genesis 26:3–4)

Isaac chose to act not on the appearance of the famine but on God's dream in faith:

> *Then Isaac sowed in that land, and received in the same year an hundredfold: and the LORD blessed him. And the man waxed great, and went forward, and grew until he became very great: for he had possession of flocks, and possession of herds, and great store of servants: and the Philistines envied him.*   (Genesis 26:12–14)

When Isaac stepped into God's promises, he stepped into abundance.

JACOB UNDERSTOOD THAT GOD'S BLESSINGS MAY BE DELAYED BUT NOT DENIED

The book of Genesis describes Isaac's son and Abraham's grandson Jacob as a nomad, wandering in the desert, without flocks and herds. He owned very little. Jacob's father, Isaac, sent him to his uncle Laban's to find a wife. Along the way, God gave Jacob a dream very similar to what He had promised to Abraham:

> *And he dreamed, and behold a ladder set up on the earth, and the top of it reached to heaven: and behold the angels of God ascending and descending on it. And, behold, the Lord stood above it, and said, I am the LORD God of Abraham thy father, and the God of Isaac: the land whereon thou liest, to thee will I give it, and to thy seed; and thy seed shall be as the dust of the earth, and thou shalt spread abroad to the west, and to the east, and to the north, and to the south: and in thee and in thy seed shall all the families of the earth be blessed.*
>
> (Genesis 28:12–14)

At the place of the vision, Jacob set up a pillar and anointed it. He renamed the city Bethel, which means "house of God."

> *And Jacob vowed a vow, saying, If God will be with me, and will keep me in this way that I go, and will give me bread to eat, and raiment to put on, so that I come again to my father's house in peace; then shall the LORD be my God: and this stone, which I have set for a pillar, shall be God's house: and of all that thou shalt give me I will surely give the tenth unto thee.*
>
> (Genesis 28:20–22)

Jacob continued his journey, arrived in his uncle Laban's home land, and fell in love with his cousin Rachel. After Jacob labored for seven years to marry Rachel, Laban deceived him by giving him Leah, Rachel's older sister, in marriage. Only after agreeing work another seven years was Jacob allowed to marry Rachel. continued working for Laban six more years. Yet, after a combin twenty years of labor, Jacob still owned nothing.

Now, we know that God gave the Scriptures to us for o instruction. (See 2 Timothy 3:16.) From our studies, we have se that no matter how long the delay, God will intervene and fulfill His promises. He promised to bless Jacob with the blessings of Abraham, and no one could stop Him. Although the blessings were delayed, they were not denied.

During Jacob's twenty years of labor, Laban had deceived him repeatedly and failed to fully pay him. Therefore, Jacob asked Laban to send him away to his own country with his wives and children. But, knowing that God had blessed his life because Jacob had been there, Laban asked Jacob to stay. He told Jacob to ask for anything he wanted.

> *And Jacob said, Thou shalt not give me any thing: if thou wilt do this thing for me, I will again feed and keep thy flock.*
> (Genesis 30:31)

As we will look at later, Jacob's grandfather Abraham had given a similar reply to the King of Sodom, lest the king should say, "*I have made Abram rich*" (Genesis 14:23). Explaining his agreement with Laban, Jacob continued,

> *I will pass through all thy flock to day, removing from thence all the speckled and spotted cattle, and all the brown cattle among the sheep, and the spotted and speckled among the goats: and of such shall be my hire. So shall my righteousness answer for me in time to come, when it shall come for my hire before thy face: every one that is not speckled and spotted among the goats, and brown among the sheep, that shall be counted stolen with me. And Laban said, Behold, I would it might be according to thy word.*   (Genesis 30:32–34)

Laban probably was thinking, *This will be wonderful, because I have only a small number of speckled and spotted animals.*

But while Jacob fed Laban's flocks, he took rods of green poplar, hazel, and chestnut, and carved chunks into them, so they looked spotted and speckled. He then put them into the gutters of the watering troughs where the animals would see them when they came to drink and conceive.

Where did this idea come from? Jacob needed an answer, and God had given a dream to him. Here's how Jacob described it to Rachel and Leah:

> *In breeding season I once had a dream in which I looked up and saw that the male goats mating with the flock were streaked, speckled or spotted. The angel of God said to me in the dream, "Jacob." I answered, "Here I am." And he said, "Look up and see that all the male goats mating with the flock are streaked, speckled or spotted, for I have seen all that Laban has been doing to you. I am the God of Bethel, where you anointed a pillar and where you made a vow to me. Now leave this land at once and go back to your native land."*
>
> (Genesis 31:10–13 NIV)

Here, we see that God had told Jacob that He would control the outcome of the animals' mating habits!

> *And the flocks conceived before the rods, and brought forth cattle ringstraked, speckled, and spotted. And Jacob did separate the lambs, and set the faces of the flocks toward the ringstraked, and all the brown in the flock of Laban; and he put his own flocks by themselves, and put them not unto Laban's cattle.*
>
> (Genesis 30:39–40)

So Jacob put the vision God had given to him constantly before the flocks' eyes. In this way, nothing would pollute the blessing God's provision for him.

> *And it came to pass, whensoever the stronger cattle did conceive, that Jacob laid the rods before the eyes of the cattle in the gutters, that they might conceive among the rods. But when the cattle were feeble, he put them not in: so the feebler were*

Laban's, and the stronger Jacob's. And the man increased exceedingly, and had much cattle, and maidservants, and menservants, and camels, and asses.

(Genesis 30:41–43)

Where did this increase come from? Jacob had such a multiplication of livestock that he was able to sell them and hire many servants. You see, Jacob trusted more in the provision for the vision God had given to him than he did in the payment of wages

---

God may allow some people to experience lengthy tests of character, as He did with Abraham, Isaac, Jacob, and Joseph. Eventually, however, God provided them with supernatural provision and wealth, and He will do the same for you. With long-suffering, they overcame all the obstacles to achieve their dreams.

due him after working twenty years for Laban! He trusted more in God's blessing than in his job's compensation!

Now, Laban and his sons were unhappy because of Jacob's prosperity. God commanded Jacob,

Return unto the land of thy fathers, and to thy kindred; and I will be with thee. And Jacob sent and called Rachel and Leah to the field unto his flock, and said unto them, I see your

father's countenance, that it is not toward me as before; but the
God of my father hath been with me.   (Genesis 31:3–5)

God released provision for the visions of Abraham, Isaac, and Jacob. Also remember that God's dream for Joseph was that he would be exalted and brought great wealth. Now, recall that Joseph was Jacob's son, so here we have four generations of dreamers! God fulfilled His promises to each of them, and they overflowed with financial blessings. Today, you and I should expect no less.

DO NOT TAKE ANY SHORTCUTS

In this book, we have plainly established that it is God's will for you to prosper. However, there are no shortcuts to God's blessings.

In Genesis 16, the Bible explains that Abraham and Sarah tried to speed up God's dream through a carnal plan. They decided to have Abraham lie with their maidservant, Hagar. She then bore a child, Ishmael, who later became Abraham's enemy and the forefather of the Arabs, who still hate Israel. If Abraham would have stopped there, he would have short-circuited God's plan for the lineage of Jesus Christ!

What if Jacob had taken an easier way out by eloping with Rachel instead of staying twenty years with Laban? He would not have received the flocks and extraordinary wealth God had planned for him; nor would he have had Leah as his wife, who bore the twelve tribes of Israel.

What would have happened if Joseph had decided to accept Potiphar's wife's invitation to sleep with her? (See Genesis 39–41.) He would not have had the opportunity to interpret Pharaoh's dreams and rise to power in Egypt; nor would he have held the position to provide for his father and brothers in the famine.

You see, shortcuts are not short in the long run!

Abraham, Isaac, Jacob, and Joseph patiently weathered their trials in integrity with faith and obedience. Likewise, we must follow God's dream, no matter how long it takes or where it takes us. As God is true, He will not violate His own Word by using unethical, illegal, immoral, or other ungodly activities to prosper us; nor will He bless haste in the pursuit of wealth.

God may allow some people to experience lengthy tests of character, as He did with Abraham, Isaac, Jacob, and Joseph. Eventually, however, God provided them with supernatural provision and wealth, and He will do the same for you. With long-suffering, they overcame all the obstacles to achieve their dreams. Few people desire long-suffering. However, none lives above the laws of God's Word. If we want to achieve our dreams, we must patiently endure His tests with obedience and faith. Even after landing in financial ruin or bankruptcy, many have bounced back to the pinnacle of success. God can do *anything* through us when we follow Him!

Resolve in your heart that nothing on earth can defeat you. Jesus has made you more than a conqueror! (See Romans 8:37.) Make decisions that align it with the Word of God. If God is not in agreement with an action, then don't do it! Press in beyond the natural limits that turn away the weak and faltering. Hold fast to the truth. Then watch God prove His every Word!

> *And we desire that every one of you do show the same diligence to the full assurance of hope unto the end: that ye be not slothful, but followers of them who through faith and patience inherit the promises.* (Hebrews 6:11–12)

This earth and everything in it is are your promises! Take charge and seize every day as if it is the last one you have. Live knowing that God will fulfill His dream in you.

DO NOT SETTLE FOR LEFTOVERS

It is interesting to study the lives of Abraham, Isaac, Jacob, and Joseph. We find that each generation lost everything, and the leftovers of God's promises did not pass from one generation to the next. Without help from forebears, they each had to start over to seize his own promises from God. They had to begin from zero to move into abundance. To receive divine inheritances, each had a personal encounter with God and came to know Him. This activated God's promises, which then manifested in their lives.

Today many people try to live on the revelation of someone else's experience with God. They see God's provision for others and hope to receive the overflow. However, the runoff from someone else's experience with God is not enough. You must have your

---

If you live only where you are now, you will never arrive where y could be. Your present and God's promise are two entirely differe lands. You must live beyond the land of the present and step ir the land of the promise.

---

own encounter with Him.

Also, many believe that inherited wealth is the way to riche but this is not biblically true. You see, it does not matter wheth your forefathers touched God or if you received your rightf inheritance from a blessed person; it matters only whether y touch the dream realm of God and receive His provision for your vision. If you have fully embraced God's purpose in your heart, then His very Words already have commanded the revenue to release as your provision. The blessing of "from zero to abundance" can be yours.

We must realize that we have a better covenant than Abraham, Isaac, and Jacob had. Jesus built ours upon better promises. Therefore, we should be seeing at least the beginning stages of God's promises. We should be having "speckled and spotted" experiences and not be on the payroll of someone else's value system. While there is nothing wrong with working for people, we should not let any job corrupt our beliefs or become our sole source of revenue. This is not God's plan for us, because, you see, wealth from God is created, not earned.

THE LAND OF THE PRESENT AND THE LAND OF THE PROMISE

One of the keys to releasing God's provision is what I call moving from the land of the present into the land of the promise. Abraham, Isaac, Jacob, and Joseph each stepped from his natural circumstances in the land of the present into the land of God's promises. As a result, they all walked into abundance.

Let's revisit Abraham's life for a few moments. He did not live in the land of his present but in the land of God's promise.

> By faith Abraham, when he was called to go out into a place which he should after receive for an inheritance, obeyed; and he went out, not knowing whither he went. By faith he sojourned in the land of promise, as in a strange country, dwelling in tabernacles with Isaac and Jacob, the heirs with him of the same promise. (Hebrews 11:8–9)

Most people do not know how to live in the land of promise, because it is not within immediate reach. They would prefer to live in the land of ownership—what they have now. Usually, man chooses to live in and settle for what he has instead of what God promises. These are very different things. You see, if you live only where you are now, you will never arrive where you could be. Your present and God's promise are two entirely different lands. You must live beyond the land of the present and step into the land of the promise.

By faith, Abraham lived *"in the land of promise, as in a strange country."* The land of promise is an unusual place. You can step into it only when you leave the arena of natural limitations.

Now, when Abraham journeyed into the land of promise, what did he look for? *"He looked for a city which hath founda-*

Remember, the answers for everything we need are in the voice God. In the vision God speaks to us is the provision.

tions, whose builder and maker is God" (Hebrews 11:10). H searched for a city with foundations, which God had built You see, Abraham lived in tents for a reason. It was becaus he refused to allow his hands to interfere with God's work c building a nation. From the beginning of his journey, Abraha willingly lived in temporary housing until God finished His work and provided him with a permanent residence.

In effect, Abraham obediently said, "I am a sojourner in a strange land, but I am looking for what God has promised will be mine. Until I see it, I will not settle for anything less. The God who has spoken it will perform it."

You see, God did not design your present to perform; He designed only His promise to perform. If you work at a job from now until you die, will you spend everything and have nothing significant at the end? Many people live and die never touching the purpose or the provision of God. If you settle only for life in the present, you will never live in the promise. You simply will not have enough money, time, or energy. You will lack the insight and foresight into God's plan for your life, and the wisdom to handle it.

In the New Testament, the apostle Paul stood on these truths:

> For our light affliction, which is but for a moment, worketh
> for us a far more exceeding and eternal weight of glory;
> while we look not at the things which are seen, but at the
> things which are not seen: for the things which are seen are
> temporal; but the things which are not seen are eternal.
> (2 Corinthians 4:17–18)

You must operate in life on the basis of God's promises. When you live the vision and the vision lives in you, then provision will start to flow to you. Remember, provision is for the vision.

GOD'S PURPOSE AND PROMISE ALWAYS RELEASE PROVISION

This is how Abraham, Isaac, Jacob, and Joseph not only survived their challenges but also accomplished the great visions God had designed for them and their descendants. How did Abraham start? He left a pagan worshipper's household when God spoke to him, and eventually became a wealthy man, known as the father of our faith.

Think about Isaac. He faced a terrible famine, yet after God spoke to him, he received a hundredfold harvest with flocks, herds, and many servants.

Jacob began as a vagabond in the desert, wandering, owning nothing, and leading no one. After God gave him a dream, Jacob escaped Laban's abuse, taking with him great wealth, wives, children, many servants, and a multitude of speckled-and-spotted animals.

God's dream in Joseph's heart catapulted him from a prison to a palace, from the occupation of a slave to the ruler of Egypt, second only to Pharaoh.

Let these testimonies bring hope to you. Realize that God's vision brings with it His provision. Sowing dream seeds causes everything to move on your behalf. You see, it is your dream—not the provision—that launches you on the journey to fulfillment.

When I was in business, I had a destructive mind-set at first. I thought that if I could earn enough money in business, then I could be successful in ministry. If I had the provision, then I would have the vision. However, I discovered that I had it backward, and the heavens were like brass. Finally, God broke to my spirit, saying, "You will not have enough money in the present to do what I say. You will have it only in the land of promise."

In the natural realm, the concepts God had spoken to me about my finances were unbelievable. At that time, only three people attended my church, and we met in my living room, but I had a vision for a choir, a band, a worship team, Bible schools all over the world, several thousand people worshipping God, and one thousand full-time missionaries on the mission field!

God showed me that having nothing in the present was not an indicator of what I would have in the land of promise. You see, you and I do not need anything in the present; we need only the land of promise. Abraham, Isaac, Jacob, and Joseph came from nothing into the land of promise. They followed the words God had spoken to them. Remember, the answers for everything we need are in the voice of God. In the vision God speaks to us is the provision.

What prophetic words has God said about your life? Are you following them? What vision is dawning inside you? Just as God had dreams for Abraham, Isaac, Jacob, and Joseph, He has a dream for you, too. You may say, "No, I don't have an overriding vision." Well, if you are Christian, you have the Holy Spirit within you. He knew you before you were born, and He understands the purpose of your existence. Your reason for living is no secret to the Holy Spirit. He knows the end before the beginning. Because He purposed it, who can annul it?

Listen to Him. What is the Spirit of God speaking to you from heaven? What has He said about your future? Always remember, God fights for your vision, if it is from Him. He battles for His purpose. The Spirit of God will reveal it to you and accomplish it.

You can have the heavenly provision you need. Simply step into it by obeying God. Are you willing, like Jacob, to carve something as simple as a branch and throw it into a trough, proclaiming, "Earth, I decree the dream of God to manifest"? This is radical thinking compared to today's average workaday mind-set. But we can live in a different economy—God's heavenly economy!

Dreams cost nothing, but most of us are afraid to have one because we fear failure. Until you live the vision and the vision lives in you, provision will not come. It cannot arrive, because it lacks a vision to attach itself to. Discover God's dream for you. Begin to speak to it. Then, step out from the land of the present into the land of the promise!

IT STARTS WITH YOUR IDENTITY IN GOD

God told Abraham, Isaac, and Jacob that He would bless all the families of the earth through their seed. As we discussed earlier, we know that Jesus came from their lineage. But what is the purpose of *your* existence? Jesus said that, in Christ, you are the light of the world, and through you (and other Christians) the world becomes saved. The lineage of Jesus Christ continues to bless all the people on earth through His followers.

Having a vision will cause you to soar above the obstacles of me humanity and everyday life. It's the dream that paves the way f your breakthrough.

Ye are the light of the world. A city that is set on an hill cannot be hid. Neither do men light a candle, and put it under a bushel, but on a candlestick; and it giveth light unto all that are in the house. Let your light so shine before men, that they may see your good works, and glorify your Father which is in heaven. (Matthew 5:14–16)

As believers in Christ, we say with Paul and Barnabas,

For so hath the Lord commanded us, saying, I have set thee to be a light of the Gentiles, that thou shouldest be for salvation unto the ends of the earth. (Acts 13:47)

The most meaningful matter on the face of this earth is acquiring eternal life. Everything we do outside the purposes of God is wood, hay, and stubble, which will be destroyed and burned. Paul wrote,

> *By the grace God has given me, I laid a foundation as a wise builder, and someone else is building on it. But each one should build with care. For no one can lay any foundation other than the one already laid, which is Jesus Christ. If anyone builds on this foundation using gold, silver, costly stones, wood, hay or straw [stubble], their work will be shown for what it is, because the Day will bring it to light. It will be revealed with fire, and the fire will test the quality of each person's work. If what has been built survives, the builder will receive a reward. If it is burned up, the builder will suffer loss but yet will be saved— even though only as one escaping through the flames.*
>
> (1 Corinthians 3:10–15 NIV)

Nothing anyone does—no matter how noble and wonderful—has any eternal reward unless it is purposed in God.

Our God-given dreams reflect our significance and His ordained purpose for our lives. Realize that your purpose and identity are in God. The God of Abraham, Isaac, Jacob, and Joseph is *your* God, too, and He has not changed. The same God who brought these men of faith through life-threatening tribulations will also deliver you. The same God who provided for them will provide for you. When you allow God and His vision to become your focus, you can soar beyond all economic, educational, social, ethnic, and gender limitations, plus any other kind of obstacle.

LET THE DREAM HAVE YOU

Everything Abraham, Isaac, Jacob, and Joseph put their hands to prospered. What was the secret of their success? They were dream-driven! Throughout their lives, their dreams carried them. God's visions for their lives were tied to provision.

I titled this book *Millionaire Mentality*, but I am actually writing about a dream mentality. I used the word *millionaire* to imply the great value of this mentality. Had I labeled it "dream mentality," you might have said, "Well, I have had dreams before." But have you really had God's dream, and has His dream had you? Until His dream has you, you don't have His dream.

Today many of us struggle to fulfill our dreams in our own strength. Instead of looking forward, we look backward, living in the present and saying, "This isn't working. It's not happening. I might as well put a stop to this dream."

No! The dream that captures your heart is your deliverance. Having a vision will cause you to soar above the obstacles of mere humanity and everyday life. It's the dream that paves the way for your breakthrough. Abraham, Isaac, Jacob, and Joseph all had the opportunity to say, "This isn't working. It's not happening. I might as well put a stop to this dream." They had nothing at the inception of their dreams, and you don't need anything, either. You need only the dream. Your provision is in the vision!

Try yielding to God's dreams and *His* strength. If we live by God's limitless words and promises, we will walk in His limitless provision.

GOD TOLD ME TO LIVE THE DREAM

When my wife, Faye, and I were going through a divorce, prayed in the Holy Spirit, and God gave a vision to me. I saw fields of people—hundreds of thousands of people—come to Jesus. Then, Jesus spoke to me, saying, "I have called you to reap the fields of the world."

At that time, my wife was suing me in divorce court. I told God, "You have one big problem." I had recently read the Scripture *"For if a man know not how to rule his own house, how shall he take care of the church of God?"* (1 Timothy 3:5), and, according to this verse, the vision was not probable.

But then God answered me, saying, "If you will live the dream I have given to you, I will run your household!"

"That's a deal," I quickly responded, "because what I'm doing isn't working at all." I had done everything to save my marriage, but nothing had worked.

The truth is that the dream from God reconciled our marriage and delivered our home. When Faye and I remarried, I told her, "Do you realize that we are not remarrying for each other? We are remarrying for the fields of the world, so that God may touch them." You see, marriage was a provision for the dream. The dream became our driving force. It was our call to His purpose.

Have you ever seen someone face miserable circumstances when engaged in God's vision for his life? Did he drop the dream because the present became too frustrating? Did you watch him lose his joy, momentum, motivation, and finances? Perhaps he lost almost everything of value. Why? It was probably because anything outside his dream would not work for him.

Again, we must understand that man does not live by bread alone but by every word that proceeds from the mouth of God. (See Deuteronomy 8:3.) Live by what God says. Let His dream drive you. If you trust in your arm of the flesh—what you can do—the Bible says that you will be cursed. However, if your trust is in God, He will bless you.

Thus saith the LORD; Cursed be the man that trusteth in man, and maketh flesh his arm, and whose heart departeth from the LORD. For he shall be like the heath in the desert, and shall not see when good cometh; but shall inhabit the parched places

*in the wilderness, in a salt land and not inhabited. Blessed is
the man that trusteth in the* Lord, *and whose hope the* Lord
*is. For he shall be as a tree planted by the waters, and that
spreadeth out her roots by the river, and shall not see when
heat cometh, but her leaf shall be green; and shall not be care-
ful in the year of drought, neither shall cease from yielding
fruit.*   (Jeremiah 17:5–8)

You will be like the godly man in Psalm 1. New life will start
growing and blossoming around you.

His delight is in the law of the Lord; *and in his law doth he
meditate day and night. And he shall be like a tree planted by
the rivers of water, that bringeth forth his fruit in his season;
his leaf also shall not wither; and whatsoever he doeth shall
prosper.*   (Psalm 1:2–3)

EVEN GENTILES FULFILL PROPHETIC VISION

Are you ready to allow your dream to drive your provision?
Nehemiah was. Let's look at his touching story now, about the
Holy Spirit's infiltration in His people's lives to restore their vision
and purpose. God gave Nehemiah a dream to rebuild Jerusalem's
walls, which had been destroyed by Israel's enemies in previous
years.

Nehemiah, whose name means "comfort of Jehovah," was a
Jewish captive of a Gentile king named Artaxerxes. He held the
trusted position of the king's personal cupbearer, which indicated
his strong character and integrity. However, his dream moved him
beyond his temporal environment and responsibilities:

*The words of Nehemiah the son of Hachaliah. It came to pass
in the month of Chislev, in the twentieth year, as I was in
Shushan the citadel, that Hanani one of my brethren came*

with men from Judah; and I asked them concerning the Jews who had escaped, who had survived the captivity, and concerning Jerusalem. And they said to me, "The survivors who are left from the captivity in the province are there in great distress and reproach. The wall of Jerusalem is also broken down, and its gates are burned with fire." So it was, when I heard these words, that I sat down and wept, and mourned for many days; I was fasting and praying before the God of heaven. (Nehemiah 1:1–4 NKJV)

---

recognize grace intervening in my life when my dream and sion are far beyond my human ability and God shows up to do it imself! I am able only to shout with Him, because I cannot make happen in my own strength.

Sometimes, dreams affect you. You start noticing chasms, ocial ills, pain, destruction, and injustices in your environment. What you see often grips your heart and moves you to tears. Take note when this happens to you, because these are the earmarks of God's vision within you. As you read the remaining portion of this tory, think about what grips your heart and moves you to tears. his happened to Nehemiah, and after, He prayed to God:

I pray, LORD God of heaven, O great and awesome God, You who keep Your covenant and mercy with those who love You and observe Your commandments, please let Your ear be attentive and Your eyes open, that You may hear the prayer of Your servant which I pray before You now, day and night,

*for the children of Israel Your servants, and confess the sins
of the children of Israel which we have sinned against You.
Both my father's house and I have sinned. We have acted very
corruptly against You, and have not kept the commandments,
the statutes, nor the ordinances which You commanded Your
servant Moses.*   (Nehemiah 1:5–7 NKJV)

One day when Nehemiah was fulfilling his role as cupbearer,
King Artaxerxes saw his unusual countenance and asked him:

*"Why is your face sad, since you are not sick? This is noth-
ing but sorrow of heart." So I became dreadfully afraid, and
said to the king, "May the king live forever! Why should my
face not be sad, when the city, the place of my fathers' tombs,
lies waste, and its gates are burned with fire?" Then the king
said to me, "What do you request?" So I prayed to the God
of heaven. And I said to the king, "If it pleases the king, and
if your servant has found favor in your sight, I ask that you
send me to Judah, to the city of my fathers' tombs, that I may
rebuild it." Then the king said to me (the queen also sitting
beside him), "How long will your journey be? And when will
you return?" So it pleased the king to send me; and I set him
a time. Furthermore I said to the king, "If it pleases the king,
let letters be given to me for the governors of the region beyond
the River, that they must permit me to pass through till I come
to Judah, and a letter to Asaph the keeper of the king's forest,
that he must give me timber to make beams for the gates of the
citadel which pertains to the temple, for the city wall, and for
the house that I will occupy." And the king granted them to
me according to the good hand of my God upon me.*
                                                  (Nehemiah 2:2–8 NKJV)

Provision came when vision penetrated Nehemiah's spirit.
In effect, he said to the Gentile king, "I have a vision, and I want
you to do something about it." What did the king do? He gave

Nehemiah all the materials necessary to finish the entire job of rebuilding the wall around Jerusalem. When you obey God and let His dream drive you, your provision may come from the most unlikely places.

LIKE ZECHARIAH, YOU WILL RECEIVE GRACE FROM GOD

The last story I want to share in this chapter is that of another builder, Zerubbabel. God gave Zerubbabel a dream of rebuilding the temple of Jerusalem. Prophet Zechariah shared the Word from God:

> This is the word of the LORD to Zerubbabel: "Not by might nor by power, but by My Spirit," says the LORD of hosts. "Who are you, O great mountain? Before Zerubbabel you shall become a plain! And he shall bring forth the capstone with shouts of 'Grace, grace to it.'" (Zechariah 4:6–7 NKJV)

Would Zerubbabel have to struggle to achieve his goal? Oh, no! Here, the Spirit of God promised to accomplish the vision with shouts of grace!

What is grace? Where does it come from, and how does it work? How can you know when you are operating in it? Some have said that grace is God's riches at Christ's expense. I recognize grace intervening in my life when my dream and vision are far beyond my human ability and God shows up to do it Himself! I am able only to shout with Him, because I cannot make it happen in my own strength.

Let's continue our study on how the Holy Spirit worked with Zerubbabel, according to the prophet Zechariah:

> The hands of Zerubbabel have laid the foundation of this temple; His hands shall also finish it. Then you will know that the LORD of hosts has sent Me to you. For who has despised the

day of small things? For these seven [eyes of the Lord] *rejoice to
see the plumb line in the hand of Zerubbabel. They are the eyes of
the* Lord, *which scan to and fro throughout the whole earth.*
(Zechariah 4:8–10 nkjv)

Zerubbabel ran with God's vision to restore Solomon's temple.
Dare I say that if you can tap into God's desires, you will never
know a day of loss or lack in your life? You will accomplish your
dream and vision not by your might or power but by His Spirit. It
will be by His grace, not by the work of man's flesh or mind. Step
over the threshold right now, and proclaim, "I am a dream-driven
believer. The dream seeds, which God has sown within my spirit,
are literally causing provision to follow me!"

Pray this with me now as we close this chapter on provision:

God,

I pray that I would become dream-led. Move me with
Your prophetic vision and purpose like You did for
Nehemiah. Release me from the influences of anything
that would bind and restrain.

Mind of God, I yield to You and submit to Your dreams
and visions. I believe that Your vision will release provision in my life. Like Abraham, Isaac, Jacob, and Joseph, I
let You multiply me.

Like Zerubbabel, I build Your vision with a capstone of
grace, for I know that it is accomplished not by might nor
by power but by Your Spirit.

Hallelujah! I cry "grace" to it. In Jesus' name, amen.

8

TAP INTO HEAVEN'S WEALTH

Now, we have seen that your dreams, perspective, actions, and words are of utmost significance if you are to engage God's provision in your life. This last chapter will give you several additional secrets to help you tap into heaven's wealth.

UNLOCK FINANCIAL RESULTS

In previous chapters, we examined Abraham's relationship with God. In our study, we saw that he obeyed God, received His promise when Sarah conceived and bore Isaac, and became extremely wealthy. Abraham knew God as his Provider:

> And the king of Sodom said unto Abram, Give me the persons, and take the goods to thyself. And Abram said to the king of Sodom, I have lift up mine hand unto the LORD, the most high God, the possessor of heaven and earth, that I will

> *not take from a thread even to a shoelatchet, and that I will*
> *not take any thing that is thine, lest thou shouldest say, I*
> *have made Abram rich.* (Genesis 14:21–23)

Remember, Abraham's grandson Jacob had said something similar to Laban. No one could rightly say that Laban made Jacob rich—only God could have performed such a miracle.

We must grasp how Abraham unlocked the financial blessings he experienced. We will examine the four keys Abraham used to release his blessing. The first of Abraham's key is having an absolute resolve that God created everything in existence. The second is believing that God owns the heavens and earth and everything in them. The third key is one of action: giving to God one-tenth of all one has and all that one receives. The fourth key is knowing how to withdraw from God's heavenly bank account. This study of Abraham will reveal awesome truths, which few have fully experienced.

1. BELIEF THAT GOD CREATED EVERYTHING IN EXISTENCE

In chapter 4, "Activate Your Dream Seeds," we studied th first chapter of Genesis, which opens our eyes to the creativ power of God's spoken words. The very words from God's mout create things.

If we applied this truth to our personal lives, we would liv unlimitedly. For example, let's say that during a quiet one-o one prayer time, you hear God speak to your spirit that He fully supplying all your needs according to Philippians 4:19: "B my God shall supply all your need according to his riches in glo by Christ Jesus." This Word would bring confidence and suppor because you would know that you cannot provide for yourself God can.

However, most people stop right there. If the fulfillment does not come immediately, they stop believing for it. Do not stop! God has purposed that rhema Word to manifest more than what meets your needs. Yes, *"according to his riches in glory"* means much more than your sustenance. Your blessing is not according to your need but according to His riches! Pray and ask your heavenly Father to reveal this truth to you. Remember the words of Jesus:

> *Then said Jesus to those Jews which believed on him, If ye continue in my word, then are ye my disciples indeed; and ye shall know the truth, and the truth shall make you free.*
>
> (John 8:31–32)

When we focus on a certain Scripture by reading, believing, and speaking it to ourselves over and over, we will receive revelation knowledge from the Lord. Ultimately, the manifestation of the Word will come.

2. GOD OWNS THE HEAVENS AND EARTH AND EVERYTHING IN THEM

With this primary thought in mind, we must conclude that we are only stewards and not the Owner. Abraham had a clear understanding of this truth. After he won a battle against those who stole his nephew Lot's wives, children, and goods, he refused to identify with a human reward system:

> *And he brought back all the goods, and also brought again his brother Lot, and his goods, and the women also, and the people. And the king of Sodom went out to meet him after his return from the slaughter of Chedorlaomer, and of the kings that were with him, at the valley of Shaveh, which is the king's dale....And the king of Sodom said unto Abram, Give me the persons, and take the goods to thyself. And Abram said to the*

king of Sodom, I have lift up mine hand unto the LORD, the most high God, the possessor of heaven and earth, that I will not take from a thread even to a shoelatchet, and that I will not take any thing that is thine, lest thou shouldest say, I have made Abram rich: save only that which the young men have eaten, and the portion of the men which went with me, Aner, Eshcol, and Mamre; let them take their portion.

(Genesis 14:16–17, 21–24)

Here, we see that Abraham clearly knew that he would become very wealthy, and he saw only one Source! Everything he had came from God.

3. GIVE TO GOD ONE-TENTH OF ALL YOU HAVE AND ALL YOU RECEIVE

This key is absolutely critical. It is not only a physical act but a heart act.

First, let's discuss the difference between tithes and offerings. Simply put, a tithe (which means a tenth or 10 percent) is one tenth of all your revenue. Notice that it is the first one-tenth, or one-tenth of your entire income, before any is taken out or used. When you pay your tithe, it must be from your firstfruits. In the Old Testament, the firstfruits were the first part of the harvest. Your tithes must not come from leftovers.

On the other hand, offerings are anything you give above and beyond the first one-tenth. I will not go into much detail about the differences; many other authors have excellent books on this topic if you want to explore more.

The act of paying tithes began before the law was given to Moses. Abraham paid tithes to Melchizedek. (See Hebrews 7:2.) Furthermore, we learned earlier that Abraham's grandson Jacob also vowed to tithe in Genesis 28:22. Today, God's Word still commands us to tithe.

Look at the following account of the covenant meal Abraham shared with Melchizedek after defeating King Chedorlaomer of Elam and the other kings aligned with him. Here, they communed and enjoyed a singleness of heart. Abraham felt a true connection to God through giving.

> *And Melchizedek king of Salem brought forth bread and wine: and he was the priest of the most high God. And he blessed him, and said, Blessed be Abram of the most high God, possessor of heaven and earth: and blessed be the most high God, which hath delivered thine enemies into thy hand. And he gave him tithes of all.* (Genesis 14:18–20)

Now, Melchizedek was not like any man, but he was like the Son of God Himself. In fact, in Hebrews 7:8, the Bible states that, on earth, men who die receive your tithes, but God also receives them in heaven:

> *For this Melchisedec, king of Salem, priest of the most high God, who met Abraham returning from the slaughter of the kings, and blessed him; to whom also Abraham gave a tenth part of all; first being by interpretation King of righteousness, and after that also King of Salem, which is, King of peace; without father, without mother, without descent, having neither beginning of days, nor end of life; but made like unto the Son of God; abideth a priest continually. Now consider how great this man was, unto whom even the patriarch Abraham gave the tenth of the spoils....And here men that die receive tithes; but there he receiveth them, of whom it is witnessed that he liveth. And as I may so say, Levi also, who receiveth tithes, payed tithes in Abraham.* (Hebrews 7:1–4, 8–9)

Realize that you pay your tithes directly to God Himself. Today, many believers dispute the practice of tithing. This is very unfortunate, because God's Word declares that we must honor Him with the first tenth of everything (before paying any bills, etc.). Otherwise, all our money is cursed. It is far better to have a blessed 90 percent than a cursed 100 percent. Look with me at the book of Malachi:

Your heart and your treasure are tied closely together. Jes explained that we can do only one of two things: trust in God a honor Him with our heart attitude and actions of giving, or trust something else as our source of financial sustenance.

Will a man rob God? Yet ye have robbed me. But ye say, Wherein have we robbed thee? In tithes and offerings. Ye are cursed with a curse: for ye have robbed me, even this whole nation. Bring ye all the tithes into the storehouse, that there may be meat in mine house, and prove me now herewith, saith the LORD of hosts, if I will not open you the windows of heaven, and pour you out a blessing, that there shall not be room enough to receive it. And I will rebuke the devourer for your sakes, and he shall not destroy the fruits of your ground; neither shall your vine cast her fruit before the time in the field, saith the LORD of hosts. And all nations shall call you blessed:

for ye shall be a delightsome land, saith the LORD of hosts.
(Malachi 3:8–12)

You must understand the phrase *"that there may be meat in mine house"* in light of the New Testament. Jesus explained what God meant: *"Jesus saith unto them, My meat is to do the will of him that sent me, and to finish his work"* (John 4:34). In other words, you give your tithes and offerings so that the church can do the will of God on earth.

Jesus also said, *"For where your treasure is, there will your heart be also"* (Matthew 6:21). Your heart and your treasure are tied closely together. Jesus explained that we can do only one of two things: trust in God and honor Him with our heart attitude and actions of giving, or trust in something else as our source of financial sustenance. Many live bound and cursed, because they trust their skills, education, retirement, or jobs for their livelihood. Proud "self-made" men, they trust their savings, stocks, bonds, or even themselves.

Our Lord continued in this passage,

For where your treasure is, there will your heart be also. The light of the body is the eye: if therefore thine eye be single, thy whole body shall be full of light. But if thine eye be evil [or covetous], thy whole body shall be full of darkness. If therefore the light that is in thee be darkness, how great is that darkness! No man can serve two masters: for either he will hate the one, and love the other; or else he will hold to the one, and despise the other. Ye cannot serve God and mammon.
(Matthew 6:21–24)

Here, Jesus warned us not to become caught in the world's systems of false security, because, in the world, everything vanishes that we use. It is all right to have a high-paying job, savings, retirement accounts, and awesome wealth. However, we must not put your trust in these.

In the above passage, Jesus said that trusting in the security or provision of something other than God is trusting in the master called "mammon." In Jesus' era, Mammon was the name of a well-known provision god of the three pagan Babylonian, Assyrian, and Egyptian empires. These three kingdoms trusted Mammon for support and revenue, as some of us today trust in our retirement accounts, so that we will not have to work. But, obviously, the false god of Mammon did not actually provide provisions, and neither do our retirement accounts.

You might be thinking, *No, my retirement assets are safe. I have invested them in low-risk mutual funds and AAA-rated bonds. I'll be able to take it easy when it's time to retire.* On this note, Jesus made some of the most profound statements in the Word:

> *Lay not up for yourselves treasures upon earth, where moth and rust doth corrupt, and where thieves break through and steal: but lay up for yourselves treasures in heaven, where neither moth nor rust doth corrupt, and where thieves do not break through nor steal.* (Matthew 6:19–20)

Jesus said it. That settles it. When we store up wealth on earth, it is not safe. Thieves can steal it, and it can wither away in various ways. For example, what would happen to our finances if the stock market crashed? God alone is our only security.

In relation to Jesus' bold and revealing statement that our earthly treasures can be stolen, you may wonder what the millionaire mentality is all about. You need to use money here on earth, so how do you not store it on earth? And if you store it in heaven, how can you use it on earth? This paradox has hindered man for two thousand years. How does it work?

4. LEARN TO WITHDRAW FROM GOD'S HEAVENLY BANK ACCOUNT

In the next few paragraphs, I will share key secrets that I have discovered about man's interaction with God in receiving His wealth. This is the fourth key in unlocking heaven's wealth for you.

Always remember that, according to God's Word, giving and receiving are linked together. Let's say you find a bank that pays an annual return of 300 percent in interest, and all you must do to be eligible for the 300 percent return is to open an account with a deposit and to establish that the funds are yours (for example, by providing a signature card and possibly your photo identification). Then, you would be on your way to earning interest. You would also be allowed to withdraw some of the funds from the account, provided that you first prove your identity. This is similar to depositing in and withdrawing from God's heavenly bank account.

Let's examine His Word to discover how to correctly deposit and withdraw. In this book, I emphasize the word *mentality*. Get ready for an attitude check! The following points contain attitudes, viewpoints, actions, and conversations that will influence the release of wealth from God to you.

Put God to the test to determine that He will fulfill His Word. To be certain that God will fulfill His Word, test Him. But remember, before God performs His promises, you must do your part! Let's revisit the book of Malachi:

> *Bring ye all the tithes into the storehouse, that there may be meat in mine house, and prove me now herewith, saith the* Lord *of hosts, if I will not open you the windows of heaven, and pour you out a blessing, that there shall not be room enough to receive it. And I will rebuke the devourer for your*

sakes, and he shall not destroy the fruits of your ground; nei-
ther shall your vine cast her fruit before the time in the field,
saith the LORD of hosts. And all nations shall call you blessed:
for ye shall be a delightsome land, saith the LORD of hosts.
(Malachi 3:10–12)

When you give, make sure your heart is in it. Place a demand upon the integrity of God's Word by believing that He will perform what He promised. This is not a onetime experience but a continual state of knowing in your heart that God does fulfill His Word. Then, you will not be afraid to trust Him. By experience, you will *know* that God is always faithful to you.

Give directly to God without speaking negatively. The way we give to God is usually through godly ministries. Sometimes however, these organizations disappoint us in how they handle our donations. This often causes many to unknowingly abort their own prosperity. Never, never, never speak negatively or in frustration regarding your financial gifts. Always tell God that you are giving your money to Him, and that no one on earth owes you a return on it. Your multiplied yield comes from God alone. Yes, God does use people, but you must not in your mind limit whom He can use. Earlier we learned that while we physically pay our tithes to mortal men, the Lord actually receives them.

Once you have given, guard your tongue! God is listening:

"You have spoken arrogantly against me," says the LORD. "Yet you ask, 'What have we said against you?' You have said, 'It is futile to serve God. What do we gain by carrying out his requirements and going about like mourners before the LORD Almighty? But now we call the arrogant blessed. Certainly evildoers prosper, and even when they put God to the test, they get away with it.'" Then those who feared the LORD talked

with each other, and the LORD *listened and heard.*
(Malachi 3:13–16 NIV)

In the King James Version, the last verse reads:

Then they that feared the LORD *spake often one to another: and the* LORD *hearkened, and heard it, and a book of remembrance was written before him for them that feared the* LORD, *and that thought upon his name.*   (Malachi 3:16)

Be sure to stay blessed. Remember Proverbs 18:21:

Death and life are in the power of the tongue: and they that love it shall eat the fruit thereof.

Always give liberally with an attitude of gratitude! Your attitude is very important when you give to the Lord. The apostle Paul said,

---

ver allow doubt to affect your confidence. Speak boldly that the
d alone is your source and supply!

But this I say, He which soweth sparingly shall reap also sparingly; and he which soweth bountifully shall reap also bountifully. Every man according as he purposeth in his heart, so let him give; not grudgingly, or of necessity: for God loveth a cheerful giver. And God is able to make all grace abound toward you;

> *that ye, always having all sufficiency in all things, may abound*
> *to every good work: (As it is written, He hath dispersed abroad;*
> *he hath given to the poor: his righteousness remaineth for ever.*
> *Now he that ministereth seed to the sower both minister bread*
> *for your food, and multiply your seed sown, and increase the*
> *fruits of your righteousness.)* (2 Corinthians 9:6–10)

The following verses clearly state that God freely gives riches for our enjoyment, but with these blessings He commands us to give generously:

> *Command those who are rich in this present world not to be*
> *arrogant nor to put their hope in wealth, which is so uncer-*
> *tain, but to put their hope in God, who richly provides us with*
> *everything for our enjoyment. Command them to do good, to*
> *be rich in good deeds, and to be generous and willing to share.*
> *In this way they will lay up treasure for themselves as a firm*
> *foundation for the coming age, so that they may take hold of*
> *the life that is truly life.* (1 Timothy 6:17–19 NIV)

Expect to receive. This is where many falter and are uncertain wondering, *How do I receive from God?* I believe that the *Amplified Bible* version of Philippians 4:13–19 says it best:

> *I have strength for all things in Christ Who empowers me [I*
> *am ready for anything and equal to anything through Him*
> *Who infuses inner strength into me; I am self-sufficient in*
> *Christ's sufficiency]. But it was right and commendable and*
> *noble of you to contribute for my needs and to share my dif-*
> *ficulties with me. And you Philippians yourselves well know*
> *that in the early days of the Gospel ministry, when I left*
> *Macedonia, no such church (assembly) entered into partner-*
> *ship with me and opened up [a debit and credit] account in*
> *giving and receiving except you only. For even in Thessalonica*
> *you sent [me contributions] for my needs, not only once but*

a second time. Not that I seek or am eager for [your] gift, but I do seek and am eager for the fruit which increases to your credit [the harvest of blessing that is accumulating to your account]. But I have [your full payment] and more; I have everything I need and am amply supplied, now that I have received from Epaphroditus the gifts you sent me. [They are the] fragrant odor of an offering and sacrifice which God welcomes and in which He delights. And my God will liberally supply (fill to the full) your every need according to His riches in glory in Christ Jesus.

Now, if you know that God has an account in heaven, through which you can deposit and withdraw wealth, then use it! This is what Jesus was referring to when He instructed us to lay up for ourselves treasures in heaven. This account is multiplying and is reserved for only you!

Never allow doubt to affect your confidence. Speak boldly that the Lord alone is your source and supply! God encouraged Abraham after he had tithed and declared that God would receive all the glory for making him rich:

After these things the word of the LORD came unto Abram in a vision, saying, Fear not, Abram: I am thy shield, and thy exceeding great reward.   (Genesis 15:1)

The act of receiving is to be our everyday routine. After all, did not Jesus teach us to pray for God to *"give us this day our daily bread"*? In what we know today as the Lord's Prayer, Jesus said,

After this manner therefore pray ye: Our Father which art in heaven, Hallowed be thy name. Thy kingdom come, thy will be done in earth, as it is in heaven. Give us this day our daily bread. And forgive us our debts, as we forgive our debtors. And lead us not into temptation, but deliver us from evil: for thine is

the kingdom, and the power, and the glory for ever. Amen.
(Matthew 6:9–13)

Then in the same chapter of Matthew, remember, Jesus declared, *"But seek ye first the kingdom of God, and his righteousness; and all these things shall be added unto you"* (Matthew 6:33). Every day is the time to receive!

A MOUNTAIN-MOVING TESTIMONY

Now, I have a special blessing for you. I will close this last chapter with a moving story of a Christian businessman. After this young man learned the true purpose of wealth and began to practice God's principles, his life was never the same. It can happen for you, too!

Many probably thought nothing much would become of the boy, the rebellious black sheep of his family. One book described him as "a grade school dropout," "a runaway from home at fourteen."[7] When he left home, he accepted a job in a foundry shoveling sand, and became an iron molder. His Christian parents who had trained him in the ways of the Lord, did not give up on him. Instead, they released their son to God and continued to pray for his salvation.

Two years later, at sixteen years of age, the young man accepted Jesus Christ as his personal Lord and Savior. That one decision forever changed his life *and the world.* You see this is the story of Robert Gilmour LeTourneau (1888–1969) internationally known inventor, entrepreneur, educator, and philanthropist. He has been "credited with the creation of the modern mechanized earthmoving industry."[8] This unique ma

---

7. Nels E. Stjernstrom, *The Joy of Accomplishment: A Story of Mr. R. G.* (Longview, TX: LeTourneau University, 1989), 20.
8. Ron Blue, *Splitting Heirs: Giving Money & Things to Your Children Without Ruining Their Lives* (Chicago, IL: Northfield Publishing, 2004), 148.

held almost three hundred patents and is rated as one of the top twenty inventors in history.[9] He created nearly three hundred inventions, including the individual electric motor, the electric wheel, bridge spans, the bulldozer, a forerunner to the modern earthmovers, the offshore drilling platform, and much more. He was the first major manufacturer to make welding a universally accepted process.[10] (Remember, I was once a welder in a factory!)

Many types of modern heavy earthmoving equipment owe their design to R. G. LeTourneau. His machines revolutionized the industries of heavy construction, mining, logging, land clearing, and offshore oil drilling. LeTourneau eventually operated manufacturing plants in California, Illinois, Georgia, Mississippi, and Texas.

During World War II, the LeTourneau Company built 70 percent of the earthmoving equipment that the Allies used.[11] At the height of the war, from 1942 to 1945, R. G. created "78 inventions, many of which were instrumental in helping to win the war."[12] In 1953, the Westinghouse Air Brake Company bought R. G. LeTourneau's designs and business for more than thirty million dollars.[13]

Additionally, R. G., together with his beloved wife, Evelyn, opened the LeTourneau Technical Institute in 1946, which has since grown into the widely acclaimed Christian institution

LeTourneau University, "The Machines," http://www.letu.edu/opencms/opencms/_Academics/library/museum/Machines/index.html.

. Texas State Historical Association, "LeTourneau, Robert Gilmour," https://haonline.org/handbook/online/articles/fle36.

. "The Machines."

. Ibid.

. R. G. LeTourneau, *R. G. Talks About…: The Industrial Genius, Practical ilosophy, and Christian Commitment of Robert G. LeTourneau (1888–1969)*, ed. uise LeTourneau Dick (Longview, TX: LeTourneau Press, 1985), 250.

LeTourneau University. U.S. News & World Report has ranked it as one of America's best colleges.[14]

The school began when Mom and Pop LeTourneau, as many called them, had a burden to help their factory workers and the returning GIs from World War II. Since these young people needed further education and spiritual ministry, the LeTourneaus started educational and spiritual training programs in their factories. This proved to be the forerunner of LeTourneau University, which has produced more than ten thousand alumni, who have reached out to serve God throughout the United States and fifty-five nations. This accredited Christian university offers degree programs today in engineering, technology, liberal arts, business, aviation, education, and the sciences, as well as master's programs in business administration and business management. Think about it: God produced all this from a grade-school dropout!

On the university's fiftieth anniversary in 1996, former President George Bush said of R. G. LeTourneau, "He was always willing to push the envelope. He was willing to follow his vision. Just as your namesake was committed to excellence, just as he was an innovative leader, so too has LeTourneau University become an institution known for its dedication to principles and its vision... Keep up the terrific work!"

Former President Bush had become well-acquainted with R. G. decades earlier after buying LeTourneau's first newly invented offshore drilling platforms. The former president of the United States "credits R. G.'s offshore rig with enabling him to gain the wealth and freedom to become involved in politics"! Do you realize the influence one person can have when simply following God's dream in his heart?

---

14. U.S. News & World Report, "LeTourneau University," http://colleges.usnew
rankingsandreviews.com/best-colleges/letourneau-university-3584.

Deciding to keep their priorities in order regarding money, Evelyn and R. G....

> ...established the LeTourneau Foundation and placed 90 percent of the corporation stock in the foundation, so that stock dividends went to the foundation instead of to them personally. The earnings from the foundation stock would then be used in Christian endeavors around the world.

> Resources from the Foundation enabled Evelyn to purchase five acres on Winona Lake, Indiana, where she established Camp Bethany in 1937. She enlisted students and graduates of Wheaton College to serve as counselors and speakers, one of whom was a young preacher named Billy Graham.[15]

> Years later, his son Franklin attended LeTourneau University and returned recently as the featured speaker at the class of 2000 commencement exercise.

> In the foreword of *Faith and Ingenuity: LeTourneau University's First Fifty Years*, board member Billy Graham wrote, "In my judgment, LeTourneau is one of the finest schools combining academics, Christian witness and technical expertise that I know about. LeTourneau University's great advantage lies in its philosophy of linking the academic and the spiritual with a practical approach. Led by the example of its founders, it produces 'faith at work' that permeates every course and impacts every student."[16]

In the early days, R. G. and Evelyn LeTourneau struggled with their desires to serve God full-time and build a business. At that point, God used their pastor to encourage them, who told them that God needs both businessmen and preachers. This truth

. Kenneth Reuben Durham, *Faith and Ingenuity: LeTourneau University's First Fifty Years* (Marceline, MO: Walsworth Publishing Co., 1995).
. Ibid., foreword.

transformed their lives. R. G. spent the next few decades traveling and building the kingdom of God at his own expense. Because of his earthmoving equipment, R. G. was also known as a mover of mountains.

It all began at age thirty, when he dedicated himself to be a "businessman for God." However, his love for building machines "never deterred him from what he felt was his reason for existence: to glorify God and spread the Gospel message"[17] "One of five founders of the Christian Business [Men's Committee] International,"[18] R. G. "is widely recognized…as the moving force behind bringing Christianity and the business world into a working relationship on many fronts."[19]

How did all this come about? R. G. LeTourneau attributed his rise from dropout to millionaire entirely to God. He claimed that he was foremost a Christian.

> I've always said when people ask me about the inventions I've come up with, that anything I've been able to do I credit to God Who gave me my mind…1 Corinthians 2:9 says, *"Eye hath not seen, nor ear heard, neither have entered into the heart of man, the things which God hath prepared for them that love Him."* Man can't comprehend such wonders with his natural mind—can't imagine it—but the next verse says, 'But God hath revealed them unto us by His Spirit.' So if you want to enter into the wonders of God, don't try to do it with man's natural mind, but accept God's Son as your Savior and let the Holy Spirit show you the wonders of a life in God, both for now and for eternity.[20]

Thousands of times around the world, he told audiences:

17. Blue, *Splitting Heirs*, 149.
18. LeTourneau, *R. G. Talks About…*, 252.
19. Ibid., 8.
20. Ibid., 244.

My life verse has been Matthew 6:33, *"Seek ye first the king-dom of God and His righteousness and all these things shall be added unto you."*[21]

Wherever he spoke, R. G. began his messages with statements like, "Friends, I'm just a sinner saved by grace, just a mechanic that the Lord has blessed. He saved me by grace and made me His child."

"My machines and my accomplishments," he once said, "seem mighty small when I look up into the heavens at night—and they tell me those stars are bigger than this world…and then I realize how small I am and wonder that God would send His Son to save me and help me."[22]

He spoke not only of his inventions and other matters of the business but also about how these physical things paralleled God's spiritual principles. For example, in 1948, he said,

> May I call to attention, the contrast between the Scripture story of creation and my story of earthmoving invention?
>
> I have said, "In the beginning I developed." So must every inventor, engineer and designer say, "I developed" or "I made." Even if it is an original invention in a virgin field it must be made from something that already exists….
>
> *"In the beginning God created."* See the difference in those first five words of the Bible. Man must start with something, but God began with nothing, absolute noth-ing, and *"created the heaven and the earth"* (Genesis 1:1). As we have it in the gospel of John, *"All things were made by him; and without him was not anything made that was made"* (John 1:3). So whether it be producing a world or a universe from nothing, or making man from the dust of the ground and breathing into his nostrils the breath of

1. Ibid., 246.
2. Ibid., 219.

life, or making the clod of the earth from which man was shaped, God is the Creator or Maker.

Had He begun with matter that another had provided, He would not be God. Having begun with nothing, nothing is for Him impossible. He could furnish the heavens with universes which men could discover only with the telescope and thereby picture the construction of the atom which they cannot see with a microscope.

Our best action then is to bow the knee as Job and say, *"I know that thou canst do everything"* (Job 42:2).[23]

Motivated by his love for God, R. G. LeTourneau founded missionary efforts in Liberia, west Africa, and in Peru, South America, where he personally invested millions of dollars. Because of this, countless thousands of people heard the gospel and received education and medical aid.[24]

In 1956, R. G. LeTourneau explained his views on wealth:

It doesn't make any difference how much money you have; you can only sleep in one bed at a time, and you can only wear one suit of clothes at a time, and I know you can't eat any more than I, so let's quit our worrying and remember we can't take it with us; but we can give it to the Lord's work and the Word of God says that we will have treasures in heaven, so I say we can send it on ahead and have it waiting for us when we get there.[25]

Near the end of his life, LeTourneau commented on tithing:

I've never been much of a preacher on tithing....My motto has been—Not how much of my money do I give

23. Ibid., 48.
24. LeTourneau University, "The Mission of R. G. LeTourneau," http://www.letu edu/_Academics/library/museum/Mission/.
25. LeTourneau, *R. G. Talks About...*, 148.

to God but how much of God's money do I keep for myself.

I hope you are now beginning to understand what I meant when I began by saying that I'm not much of a preacher of tithing. If under the law the people of God gave one-tenth to the Lord, shame on us living under grace, if we don't do better. The tithe may be a place to begin if you are not now giving to the Lord, but it's no place to stop. You see what I mean. If you get a vision of what our salvation cost, see Christ on the cross, the cruel nails in His hands and feet, the mocking crowd and the weight of our sin paying the penalty for you and for me, it will put your service and giving on a different plane. He gave Himself willingly to give us salvation from our sin. If this grips us, we can't help but love Him…

True love based on an understanding of God's grace, deep gratitude for the gift of salvation through our Lord will settle the problem of "what I should give to God" because my thinking will be turned around to consider that all I am and have belong to Him, and I am a steward for Him while serving Him in this life.[26]

In paying tribute to R. G. on his seventieth birthday, his son Richard recounted the Christian principles his father abided by to success:

1. First of all he has a deep desire to do the will of the Lord whatever it may be and is willing to accept the will of the Lord without question….

2. Secondly, he has a tremendous faith that the Lord will overcome all problems and difficulties in His own time and in His own manner….

. Ibid., 246–247.

3. His sole purpose in life is to serve the Lord in whatever way the Lord would have him do so....

4. In operation of the business, he believes that most men are, or at least should be, interested in the work they are doing and not just an eight to five or seven to three thirty clock puncher....

5. In dealing with personnel, he can forgive and forget a thousand-dollar mistake if the individual admits it was a mistake and makes no attempt to cover it up....

6. Lastly, to everyone who is close to him, he is one who "practices what he preaches."[27]

In a report on R. G. LeTourneau's memorial service, the *Longview News-Journal* read:

> Basing his remarks on the life of Mr. LeTourneau on Acts 13:36, Dr. Harvey said, "Robert Gilmour LeTourneau structured his life on the principles that a man must know God, a man must know the will of God, and a man must carry out the will of God. Mr. LeTourneau believed with all his heart that God had a message for him and the most fitting epitaph for this great man is that he served his generation by the will of God.
>
> His driving force was to get all men to know God as he did, for God was real to him...and he talked to God with the ease of sure knowledge, at any time and any place."[28]

After the memorial service, one of LeTourneau's employee wrote:

> How do we account for a ministry of such scope by one couple? Maybe this explains it: Mr. R. G., speaking to a men's meeting, said, "You will never know what you

27. Ibid., 9–12.
28. Ibid., 252–253.

can accomplish, what your potential is, until you say A GREAT BIG 'YES' TO GOD.".…In answer to the question of how we can know God's will for our lives, Mr. R. G. often answers, "You don't need to know that. If you have a guide Whom you trust, you do not need to know the destination to follow Him. Simply take the NEXT STEP with Him; put your trust in Him in all the details of life."[29]

In his autobiography, R. G. LeTourneau wrote:

For twenty-five years or more, I've been traveling this land of ours and a few foreign countries trying to teach and preach by word of mouth and example, that a Christian businessman owes as much to God as a preacher does. The rest of the time I build machinery, almost any kind of machinery as long as it is big, and powerful, and can move around to do things no other machine could do before. Some people think I'm all mixed up—that you can't serve the Lord and business, too, but that's just the point. God needs businessmen as partners as well as preachers. When He created the world and everything in it, He didn't mean for us to stop there and say, "God, You've done it all. There's nothing left for us to build." He wanted us to take off from there and really build for His greater glory.[30]

Upon R. G. LeTourneau's death in 1969, the *New York Times* published a story about the "internationally known manufacturer of earthmoving equipment," which included the following:

Robert Gilmour LeTourneau liked to do two things: "One is to design machines, turn on the power and see them work; the other is to help turn on the power of the

. Ibid., 239.
. R. G. LeTourneau, *R. G. LeTourneau: Mover of Men and Mountains* (Chicago, : Moody Press), 1.

gospel and see it work in people's lives." He did both in a big way.

Mr. LeTourneau was the developer and manufacturer of the world's largest earthmoving machinery. He was also a crusading evangelist who regularly traveled more than two hundred thousand miles a year preaching. His motto was "God is my partner...God is chairman of my board of directors."

Mr. LeTourneau believed that "a factory can be dedicated to God as well as a church and that it may be used as a means of saving many souls."[31]

Once R. G. LeTourneau shared a story about visiting a diamond mine in Belgiam Congo. After his visit, he received a letter from the owner asking if he had a machine that would improve the company's efficiency. As R. G. toured the operation, God gave revelation knowledge to him. He saw the diamond-mining process with spiritual eyes, and said,

> The Bible likens our work down here for the Lord, to gold, silver and precious stones. It will be tried by fire and the wood, hay and stubble will be burned up; so I want my work to be like a jewel, a diamond if you please, for the Lord....I believe God is handpicking out of this wicked world a people that will sparkle for him in the ages to come, some out of every kindred, tongue, people and nation. And they will sing a new song in heaven, Revelation 5:9.[32]

Are you a diamond for God? Will you allow Him to sparkle through you?

Remember, His purpose for your life includes prosperity not only for you but also for His kingdom's work.

---

31. LeTourneau, *R. G. Talks About...*, 248–250.
32. Ibid., 230–232.

Look for your dream seeds—those giftings or talents that God has planted in you as seeds of prophetic vision. Nurture them. Begin to pursue His vision. Become pregnant with God's dream as you meditate on it and His Word. Declare the Word and God's provision over your life. When you do, you will find God's field for you, and blessings of wealth will follow. Thus, your heavenly Father will provide the way for you to achieve His purpose and find true fulfillment. Then you can bless the work of the Lord.

Now you know the principles for obtaining a millionaire mentality. What will you do with this information? Will you allow it to change your life so you can provide for your family and become a cash pump for the kingdom of God? It's your choice. The entire world is awaiting your decision. Go for it!

APPENDIX

LIFE AS GOD'S CHILD

GROW BY BECOMING GOD'S CHILD

Have you ever received God's free gift of eternal life? Do you know for certain that if you were to die today, you would go to heaven? Everlasting life is a gift from God. When Jesus Christ physically died on the cross and rose from the grave, He paid for our sins. The Bible says:

> *For God so loved the world, that he gave his only begotten Son, that whosoever believeth in him should not perish, but have everlasting life.* (John 3:16)

Since Jesus paid for this gift, we don't have to. We need only receive it.

> *But as many as received him, to them gave he power to become the sons of God, even to them that believe on his name.* (John 1:12)

For by grace are ye saved through faith; and that not of yourselves: it is the gift of God: not of works, lest any man should boast.
(Ephesians 2:8–9)

The way to receive God's gift is simply to believe God's Word and receive it by professing it aloud.

If you declare with your mouth, "Jesus is Lord," and believe in your heart that God raised him from the dead, you will be saved. For it is with your heart that you believe and are justified, and it is with your mouth that you profess your faith and are saved.
(Romans 10:9–10 NIV)

Now, if you want to receive eternal life, pray aloud this prayer:

Father,

Thank You for loving me. Thank You for giving Your Son, Jesus, to die and to raise from the dead for me.

Jesus Christ, Son of God, come into my heart, forgive me of my sins, and be my Lord and Savior. Jesus, I declare that You are Lord and that You are Lord of my life. In Jesus' name, amen.

You are now born again!

All believers are entitled to over seven thousand promises that God has written in His Word. If you prayed this prayer, that now includes you! To learn about these promises, I encourage you to regularly attend a local church that teaches the uncompromised Word of God—the Bible.[33] Daily spend time in prayer, fellowship with the Lord, and reading the Bible. This will hel

---

33. If you are in the area of New Castle, Delaware, please join us for services at Victory Christian Fellowship. Visit our Web site, www.gwwm.com, for more information and directions.

you to understand the *"new creature"* that you have become in Christ.

> If any man be in Christ, he is a new creature: old things are passed away; behold, all things are become new.
>
> (2 Corinthians 5:17)

For more information about your new life in Christ, I encourage you to read the book *The Victorious Walk: A Handbook for the New Believer's Victory.*

GROW BY RECEIVING GOD'S SPIRIT

Have you received the Holy Spirit since you first believed? In Acts 19:2 (NKJV), the apostle Paul asked the Ephesians this very important question: *"Did you receive the Holy Spirit when you believed?"* The question startled them, and they answered, *"We have not so much as heard whether there is a Holy Spirit."*

Later, when they prayed together, *"the Holy Spirit came on them, and they spoke in tongues and prophesied"* (Acts 19:6 NIV).

WHAT IS BAPTISM IN THE HOLY SPIRIT?

Baptism in the Holy Spirit happens when God pours out His Spirit into a person's life to equip him or her to be a witness of Jesus. Christ said,

> But ye shall receive power, after that the Holy Ghost is come upon you: and ye shall be witnesses unto me both in Jerusalem, and in all Judaea, and in Samaria, and unto the uttermost part of the earth.
>
> (Acts 1:8)

Baptism in the Holy Spirit is an anointing of power, an enabling or ability from God, that equips believers to be witnesses of the life of Jesus Christ.

The Holy Spirit was given to mankind on the day of Pentecost and has never left. Baptism in the Spirit is a distinct experience from conversion to Christ. It was a separate experience in the apostles' lives on the day of Pentecost, and it is a separate experience for believers today.

WHO IS IT FOR?

The baptism in the Holy Spirit is for believers, because without Christ, the world cannot receive Him. This experience is to equip and empower believers to supernaturally worship God. The first move of the Holy Spirit when He came upon the early Christians was to praise God through them. (See Acts 2:11.)

WHY BE BAPTIZED IN THE HOLY SPIRIT?

It is God's will for every believer to be baptized in the Holy Spirit. It is His desire that you continually overflow with His Spirit. Jesus *commanded* the disciples not to leave Jerusalem until they had been endued with power.

> *And, behold, I send the promise of my Father upon you: but tarry ye in the city of Jerusalem, until ye be endued with power from on high.* (Luke 24:49)

In Ephesians 5:17–18, the Word of God says that believers are to understand (comprehend, grasp, perceive) what the will of the Lord is and to be filled with the Holy Spirit.

> *Wherefore be ye not unwise, but understanding what the will of the Lord is. And be not drunk with wine, wherein is excess; but be filled with the Spirit.*

Jesus also said that those who believe on Him should receive the Holy Spirit:

But this spake he of the Spirit, which they that believe on him should receive: for the Holy Ghost was not yet given; because that Jesus was not yet glorified. (John 7:39)

HOW DO I RECEIVE THE BAPTISM IN THE HOLY SPIRIT?

Ask, and you will receive. Knowing that it is God's will for us to be filled with the Holy Spirit gives us confidence in asking Him to baptize us in the Holy Spirit.

And this is the confidence that we have in him, that, if we ask any thing according to his will, he heareth us: and if we know that he hear us, whatsoever we ask, we know that we have the petitions that we desired of him.

(1 John 5:14–15)

Ask, and it shall be given you. (Luke 11:9)

If ye then, being evil, know how to give good gifts unto your children: how much more shall your heavenly Father give the Holy Spirit to them that ask him? (Luke 11:13)

WHAT HAPPENS WHEN I RECEIVE THE BAPTISM IN THE HOLY SPIRIT?

When you are filled with the Holy Spirit, you will speak in a supernatural language. Your heart will be turned more completely to God, with whom you were reconciled when you were born again. Jesus said, *"And these signs shall follow them that believe; in my name…they shall speak with new tongues"* (Mark 16:17).

The Gentiles in the house of Cornelius spoke in tongues when the Holy Spirit came on them. (See Acts 10:44–48.) Likewise, as we studied earlier, the people of Ephesus spoke in tongues when the Holy Spirit came upon them: *"And when Paul had laid hands on them, the Holy Spirit came upon them, and they spoke with tongues and prophesied"* (Acts 19:6 NKJV).

WHAT ARE THE BENEFITS OF SPEAKING IN TONGUES?

1. It allows us to praise the Lord in a God-appointed way.

When thou shalt bless with the spirit...thou verily givest thanks well. (1 Corinthians 14:16–17)

2. It spiritually edifies us.

He that speaketh in an unknown tongue edifieth himself. (1 Corinthians 14:4)

3. It reminds us of the Holy Spirit's indwelling presence.

And I will pray the Father, and He will give you another Helper, that He may abide with you forever—the Spirit of truth, whom the world cannot receive, because it neither sees Him nor knows Him; but you know Him, for He dwells with you and will be in you. (John 14:16–17 NKJV)

4. It helps us to pray in line with God's perfect will.

Likewise the Spirit also helpeth our infirmities: for we know not what we should pray for as we ought: but the Spirit itself maketh intercession for us with groanings which cannot be uttered. And he that searcheth the hearts knoweth what is the mind of the Spirit, because he maketh intercession for the saints according to the will of God. (Romans 8:26–27)

5. It stimulates faith.

But ye, beloved, building up yourselves on your most holy faith, praying in the Holy Ghost. (Jude 1:20)

6. It spiritually refreshes us.

For with stammering lips and another tongue will he speak to this people. To whom he said, This is the rest wherewith ye may cause the weary to rest; and this is the refreshing: yet they would not hear. (Isaiah 28:11–12)

7. It gives us direct access to God.

For he that speaketh in an unknown tongue speaketh not unto men, but unto God: for no man understandeth him; howbeit in the spirit he speaketh mysteries.
(1 Corinthians 14:2)

For if I pray in an unknown tongue, my spirit prayeth, but my understanding is unfruitful. (1 Corinthians 14:14)

If you want to receive the baptism of the Holy Spirit, please pray this prayer aloud:

Father,

Thank You that if I ask to be filled with the Holy Spirit, I will be filled. The evidence is that I will speak in other tongues by my will, though I may not understand what I'm speaking in my mind.

Now, Father, fill me with the Holy Spirit, in the name of Jesus. Thank You for filling me. I received it now. By a decision of my will, I will speak to You in other tongues. In Jesus' name, amen.

We can build ourselves up and speak to God wherever we e—in the car, on the bus or an airplane, at home, or even on the b. It will not disturb anyone. Speaking in tongues is a means of eping free from the contamination of the world.

THE SUPERNATURAL GIFTS OF THE HOLY SPIRIT

The gifts of the Holy Spirit can begin to operate in and through someone's life after he's received the Holy Spirit. According to 1 Corinthians 12:7–11, the nine gifts of the Spirit are:

+ Word of Wisdom

+ Word of Knowledge

+ Special Faith

+ Healing

+ Working of Miracles

+ Prophecy

+ Discerning of Spirits

+ Speaking in Tongues

+ Interpretation of Tongues

For more information about the gifts of the Spirit and how to live as a victorious Christian, please refer to my book *The Victorious Walk: A Handbook for the New Believer's Victory.*

GROW BY KNOWING GOD'S WORD

Become a student of God's Word. One way to do this is to enroll in a school of biblical studies. Start reading the Bible and ask the Holy Spirit to reveal God's truth to you. This is essential to living a victorious life.

Now let's take a look at our #1 enemy.

+ Our #1 enemy is on the prowl.

+ Our #1 enemy knows more than you know.

+ Our #1 enemy keeps you from complete fulfillment.

+ Our #1 enemy has destroyed your past.

+ Our #1 enemy breaks up families.

+ Our #1 enemy is always with you.

+ Our #1 enemy is (shh—don't tell anybody) ignorance!

What you *don't know* will hurt you! Don't let ignorance destroy your future like it has your past! God has declared, *"My people are destroyed for lack of knowledge: because thou hast rejected knowledge, I will also reject thee"* (Hosea 4:6).

ABOUT THE AUTHOR

Gary Whetstone is the founder and senior pastor of Victory Christian Fellowship in New Castle, Delaware, and founder of Gary Whetstone Worldwide Ministries. He holds an doctorate degree in religious education from Chesapeake Bible College & Seminary in Ridgely, Maryland.

Since personally experiencing God's miraculous deliverance and healing in 1971, Dr. Whetstone has devoted his life to helping others experience freedom through God's Word. Today, he frequently ministers around the world in churches, seminars, and evangelistic crusades. Gifted in teaching, Dr. Whetstone provides practical biblical instruction wherever he ministers and has seen God work powerful signs, wonders, and miracles in his minstry. Hundreds of thousands of people have become born-again, Spirit-led, healed, and set free.

Having a great burden to minister to the local community, Pastor Gary Whetstone and his church have launched

life-changing outreaches in several areas. These include HIV/
AIDS; substance and alcohol abuse; inner-city community outreach centers; Saturday Sidewalk Sunday School; food and clothing outreach programs; and many large evangelistic campaigns,
such as the dramatic production "Jesus, Light of the World," which
draws over forty-five thousand people annually.

Desiring to spread the truth and good news of the gospel
throughout the world, Dr. Whetstone's passion is to see the Word
of God cover the earth as the waters cover the seas. This vision
is being accomplished through many ministry outreaches. These
include sending mission and evangelism teams around the globe;
radio and television broadcasting; ministry through the Internet;
and the School of Biblical Studies. An extensive audio and video
training program, this school equips Christians to experience
God's presence and to understand the Bible. Today, this training program is established in hundreds of churches in North and
South America, Australia, Europe, Asia, and Africa. In addition
to local church and international branch locations, the School of
Biblical Studies is available to individuals by extension in their
homes using audiocassettes, videotapes, CDs, CD-ROMs, and
VCDs.

Gary Whetstone has appeared on many national and international radio and television programs, and has authored many
books, including *The Victorious Walk: A Handbook for the New
Believer's Victory, How to Identify and Remove Curses, Make Fear
Bow*, and his personal testimony of miraculous deliverance and
healing in *Conquering Your Unseen Enemies: How Jesus Sets You
Free*. The large number of study guides he has produced are a testament to his gifting in practical biblical teaching, and are available for use with his numerous video and audio teaching series.

God has gifted Dr. Whetstone with incredible business sense
and ability, enabling him to publish a series of teachings, including *Purchasing and Negotiations* and *Success in Business*, which

has aired on his radio program Power Impact. This broadcast currently has an audience of over four million listeners on the East Coast of the United States.

Dr. Whetstone and his wife of nearly thirty years, Faye, have a unique testimony of a restored marriage, which achieved national attention and was the cover story in Charisma magazine. Gary and Faye now conduct annual Marriage Advance seminars for couples looking to deeply enrich their relationships.

Their two adult children, Eric and Laurie, along with daughter-in-law, Rebecca, and grandson, Isaiah, are actively involved in local and international outreaches for Jesus Christ. To arrange a speaking engagement for Gary or Faye Whetstone, please contact:

Gary Whetstone Worldwide Ministries
P.O. Box 10050
Wilmington, DE 19850
E-mail: info@gwwm.com

Welcome to Our House!

We Have a Special Gift for You

It is our privilege and pleasure to share in your love of Christian books. We are committed to bringing you authors and books that feed, challenge, and enrich your faith.

To show our appreciation, we invite you to sign up to receive a specially selected **Reader Appreciation Gift**, with our compliments. Just go to the Web address at the bottom of this page.

God bless you as you seek a deeper walk with Him!

WE HAVE A GIFT FOR YOU. VISIT:

whpub.me/nonfictionthx

WHITAKER
HOUSE